VOICES OF Impact

EMPOWERING STORIES FROM FEMALE VISIONARIES AND ENTREPRENEURS

Voices of Impact Publishing

Foreword by Melanie Wood

Stories are the most powerful way to have an impact and create a ripple effect in this world.

I have worked with hundreds of women to gain Clarity and Confidence in sharing their stories on stage, on podcasts, at summits and more.

An opportunity came to me early in 2022 to create this book series to share transformational stories of women making an impact.

Sharing my own story in 2020 in a book series and becoming a best-selling author was a game changer. It was time to give this opportunity to other women to make an impact.

It began as something I'd never set out to do; I wasn't born a speaker, a leader or a business owner. Throughout my life, public speaking was never on my horizon. I would avoid it throughout school and my career for almost thirty years – and I did well to avoid it at all costs!

Not setting out to do what I do today came from one of my biggest challenges back in my late teens and early 20s. I was in an abusive marriage where I lost my confidence, voice, certainty, my way in life, and who I was as a woman to the point that I didn't want to be here.

Then one day, a person came along and gave me hope. She reached out to me on a day I couldn't hide anymore what I was going through, and she asked if I was okay, and for once, I said, "No." I knew I had to be ok with using my voice and what would happen next. Her "Impact" on my life is why I'm here today and why I'm so passionate about sharing stories.

As she shared her own story, it gave me hope and the support I needed to leave that marriage. After meeting her and the years that followed, I knew that I was here for more to help other women overcome challenges and find their voice, confidence, and certainty around who they are.

Life changed for me one day 9 yrs ago; an opportunity to come to Australia for a year, and something within told me it was time for my adventure to begin, which was what I had been waiting for. Before leaving, I was given the book "The Secret" by Rhonda Byrne. Which changed the way I viewed the world at that moment.

Arriving in Australia, I was ready! Ready to take action! Even though I was scared of being in a new country, I built my new life to stay permanently in Australia.

I wanted to help women like you (that amazing lady reading this book!) have a voice, confidence and clarity. To be able to use your authenticity to create and build a skill set for you and your business and your life or represent your organisation through storytelling, public speaking and communication.

I started my business, Speaking Styles, five years ago and have worked with hundreds of women to help them have a voice in this world to share their story, their message, and their value. To be heard and understood in this world and create a ripple effect, as I believe that stories are how we save lives, make a change, heal ourselves, and help heal other people—giving them hope and permission to do the same.

Building my business for the past 5yrs and working with women is because I knew how to use speaking to create an impact and attract clients. Out of my past experience, I understand what it's like to be in my client's shoes to have empathy and authenticity to work and guide them through sharing their stories.

Doing this work didn't come without its challenges; over 2 years ago, I was 3 days out from living in my car when the big C hit; 6 months before that, I was in debt and struggling to have enough money for rent and food.

I knew these challenges and feelings were part of who I was becoming and where I would be of service in this world—being heartfelt and authentic in everything I do. I didn't get here on my own; yes, I've done the work of the people who have worked with me and guided me over the past 5yrs, and without them, this wouldn't be possible.

I know in my heart that sharing stories is how we create change and save the lives of others, heal ourselves and rise up us all as a collective.

By sharing your story, by communicating your message, by communicating your fantastic work, experience, and expertise, no matter what field you are in. Just like the women in this book are sharing.

At the beginning of the year of 2022, I had this burning desire to create a new opportunity for women to share their transformational stories and IMPACT the world on a larger scale and reach more people. Then one day, only a few months ago, that opportunity came knocking, and Voices of Impact was born, and that desire came to light.

In Volume 1 of Voices of Impact 25 women said yes to being published authors, and it has been an absolute pleasure to publish incredible women's transformational stories. Now continuing the journey in our next volume, shining a light on more incredible women sharing stories of hope, permission and transformation.

In Volume 2 of Voices of Impact, you will read 20 Visionary Women from around the world sharing TRANSFORMATIONAL stories, creating change and a ripple effect in this WORLD.

In Volume 3 of Voices of Impact, you will read 24 Entrepreneurial and Visionary Women. Through their personal journeys of transformation, they have all stepped up with a Powerful Message to create an Impact in their lives, businesses and the lives of others.

In this volume 5 of Voices of Impact, you will read from 13 Entrepreneurial and Visionary Women, sharing incredible inspirational stories of bravery, courage and determination to overcome and become the best versions of themselves to IMPACT the world.

****

Change is within each of us, waiting to be heard and understood.

Ladies, it's your time to step up, step out and lead the change!

The world needs to hear your story!

IMPACT starts with you. Are you with me?

Melanie Wood
Founder, Speaker, Author, Publisher
Voices of Impact Publishing

****

Would you love to have your voice heard to share your story?

Reach out x

melanie@speakingstyles.com.au

Contents

Diane Armstrong

Borrowed Light. Earned Belief.

"There's a crack in everything. That's how the light gets in."

~ Leonard Cohen

What if the moments that feel the most broken aren't the end of the story, but the start of a different one?

I didn't understand that at first. Not with words. I understood it with light. When it hit, it was like a shockwave to the very essence of my being.

Standing on a southern New South Wales beach at sunrise, I was surrounded by other photographers. It was my first trip away since separating from the man I had devoted my life to. Everyone was waiting expectantly for THE moment. That perfect shot. The shot that makes you feel like you've captured something rare.

But as I stood there, sand etching between my toes, I realised I wasn't waiting for the perfect photo. I was waiting for the moment my life stopped hurting.

The hurt had become ordinary. Almost comfortable. It sat in my chest like a heavy load, something I'd learnt to live with. But in my mind, the hurt and trauma I knew like a friend had to shift. I remember thinking, how much can one person bear before they change completely?

My camera sat on its tripod, precariously close to the waterline, while the waves washed gently underneath. The sky was quiet, clouds diffused, the sun pushing through softly. It was a pale dawn, the kind photographers sometimes dismiss as nothing special, but the glow touched the trees, glistened on the sand, and the light shifted my focus. While the view that morning was spectacular, I didn't see its true beauty until later.

Photography has a way of slowing time. It asks you to wait, to observe, and notice what's happening beyond the obvious. As I watched the light move across the landscape, I felt something stir inside me. It wasn't excitement. It was more muted. It was recognition. I didn't know it then, but I was learning how to see beyond what was in front of me, and through that, how to begin again.

I had incredible opportunities growing up. I'm forever grateful for a family that gave me moments to learn, to shine, to excel, and to be myself.

My Nanna was a light, a glow that felt comfortable. Even now, I can picture her sponge cake with jam and cream, cut with a circle in the middle and wedges out from that like pure magic. I always got the inner circle with no hard edges. I felt special around her, and the way she made me feel still shapes me every day.

My dream was to be like that. To have a family of my own and be that same warmth for them. It wasn't even really a dream. It was ingrained in every cell.

But I had to let the light in through the cracks.

For most of my life, I didn't listen to myself. I hadn't learnt how. I didn't think things through before acting. I took every new opportunity by the horns and jumped right in. My adventurous spirit was how I achieved, and I was proud of it. I moved from one challenge to the next out of necessity, and it never felt wrong.

I married young to a man who was the apple of my eye. I felt whole with him and excited to start our adventure together. But moving away from my birth family was one of the hardest challenges of my life. My new family, caring in-laws, welcomed me into their world in remote Central Queensland, where roads were corrugated dirt, and the highway dropped away sharply at the sides. Back then it felt like the end of the earth. Meeting a road train on the narrow road wasn't an inconvenience; it was an event, and a hazard I knew well.

Of course, it's not classed as remote now, but at the time it truly felt like the edge of nowhere. Going into town was a once-a-fortnight necessity unless urgent parts had to be collected. The final stop was always Primac (Elders), checking there were no other errands before the long trip home. If anything went wrong, there were no mobile phones back then.

Life did what life does. It moved forward in stages.

We had four beautiful sons. We built a business that survived a wild ride of good times and bad, droughts, floods, and a volatile economy that didn't care how tired you are. It grew, and we grew with it.

When the boys reached high school age, after years of driving and running a school bus to the local school, we had to decide what came next. Boarding school became our reality, and life shifted again. More survival and change. School offered the boys opportunities for sport, teamwork, and leadership.

But their absence created a void, and I became vigilant to the changes around me.

My heart ached seeing their pain. I longed to have my children back in the circle of my arms, back under familiar routines, back beneath the vast sky that felt like it embraced you daily, and back in the safety of the open space of our farm.

I learnt to trust my instincts. To anticipate a shift in dynamics. To sense when something was about to change. At the time, I didn't call it intuition. It happened without thinking. Now I know what it was. Endurance.

What I didn't realise was that this way of seeing, this awareness, would become the foundation of my art. It was the beginning of something else. The ability to see the light in the cracks.

Cracked But Not Broken

The man I'd spent a lifetime loving no longer wanted to be part of my life. Everything I knew changed. One moment I believed we were heading towards the life we'd planned, and the next I was watching it collapse. It was soul-destroying.

We'd worked side by side for 36 years, building our family, our business, and our farm from scratch. Our roles were woven together, partners in life and partners in work. I thought we'd grow old together. Even in the volatile years, I clung to the belief that we'd find our way through. When it ended, I didn't just lose a relationship. I lost the future I'd pictured, the identity I'd lived inside, and the sense of belonging that had once felt permanent.

After that, nothing felt familiar. The structure of a life built over decades was gone, and I found myself standing in a space I wasn't prepared for, who am I?

Nothing prepares you for the moment your identity disappears. I had no map and no idea how to move forward. Trauma and shock engulfed me. There's a particular kind of silence that follows loss, and it isn't peaceful. For the longest time it echoed loudly, and my questions went unanswered.

- What do I love?

- What do I believe?

- Who am I now?

- How do I move through the loss of family, community, and certainty?

I was forced to slow down and look at my life. I didn't realise that's what was happening at the time. It was survival.

I learnt to forgive, slowly. I learnt to breathe, slowly. As COVID restrictions relaxed, I began to rebuild. I had time to volunteer. Time to meet people. I sought help and guidance, and my friends and family went above and beyond.

These words echoed in my head. *'I know what I'm doing. I've got a plan for you, plans to take care of you, not to abandon you, plans to give you the future you hope for.'* Jeremiah 29:11

A friend recently said something else that lodged in my mind. *'In the days when you had no deeper to fall and had to look up, no way could you ever have imagined blooming after the desert years.* That's how it felt. Desert years. Stripped back to nothing.

Asking For Help is Strength

For a long time, I held the inherited belief that needing help was a weakness. After loss, we can become more sensitive to asking for help and relying on others. I thought coping was something I had to do quietly, alone, shoulders squared, feelings packed away neatly where no one could see them. I was wrong.

The magnitude of what had taken place over the last decade took its toll. I learnt quickly how much I needed others, and how much they could inspire me. There were times I felt like a burden. I'll always be grateful for the heavy lifting my support team, old friends, new friends, and family did in those early years.

In the fragile space between who I'd been and who I was becoming, there were people who stepped in without trying to fix me. They didn't demand explanations or timelines. They didn't need me to be confident or certain, even though I expected that of myself. I had to let go of that and accept what they offered. Steady, unspoken, and mostly patient belief. They held the light for me when mine was only a dim flicker.

I also had a professional team that was crucial. You need that. My old GP cried when she learnt I was now on my own. It didn't remove the devastation, but her relief reminded me that my life mattered. That what I was carrying wasn't small. That I wasn't being dramatic. I was rebuilding after the ground had collapsed under me.

Finding new people for every little thing seemed stressful, but I'm deeply grateful for the people God placed in my path: doctors, psychologists, hairdressers, beauticians, all people with real compassion.

Some were mentors who saw my potential long before I did. I can't understate how important it was to try new things, join clubs, take courses, and take risks that expanded my world when my instinct was to shrink.

Others were friends who reminded me, sometimes gently, sometimes firmly, that my voice mattered, my presence mattered, and my work mattered.

They allowed space for my creativity to build. One gave up her space so my first exhibition could happen. They showed up, encouraged me, and shared my work. They spoke my name in rooms I hadn't even entered. They believed in the direction I was walking even when I wasn't sure where I was going.

Belief didn't arrive with a bang. It still isn't easy. I know the magnitude of the earthquake that rocked my world wasn't going to disappear neatly.

Small gestures matter more than people realise. A message at the right moment. An invitation. A quiet affirmation when doubt creeps in. These moments accumulate. They build scaffolding around a fragile sense of self until it becomes strong enough to stand on its own. I let borrowed belief carry me for a long time.

I'm not ashamed of that.

Sometimes we need others to see clearly until we can see ourselves again. Yes, it felt like a rescue, but it was also a witness. One day, I hope I can be that witness for someone else.

Surrounding yourself with people who reflect your potential back to you is essential, especially when you're rebuilding, especially when you're learning who you are underneath an old identity. I wanted to be a wife, a mother, and a loved Nanna, just like mine was to me. I thought that dream had been destroyed.

Eventually, life began to shift… again. Borrowed belief grew roots, like a tree ravaged by drought or fire that somehow pushes new green life out again.

Internally, I began to recognise a small candle of light. A strength that started to beam so strongly that no one could extinguish it. For the first time in years, I recognised I had a voice. I had the authority to make decisions on my own. I wouldn't be where I am now without those who held the light steady while I learnt to trust my own glow.

It begins with community, people who walk beside you rather than ahead of you. It was a turning point as I stepped outside my comfort zone. Reinvention.

Looking back, there were milestones where an internal shift took place. I set boundaries to protect myself from continued, endless hurt, the kind that can eat away at you if you let it. I'm not saying the sadness disappears. I wouldn't be who I am if it didn't have a place in me. It's about acceptance, forgiveness, trust, and lots of it.

Someone close to me said, *'Just go and do what you want to do'*. It hurt because all I wanted was my family back the way it had been. But it also set something in motion.

Healing turned into courage. Courage turned into action. Action turned into contentment.

Life's about taking risks and accepting you might fail. Fear of failure is real, but where would we be without risk? I've never been sure whether being adventurous is always a good thing. I accept challenges without thinking through the workload or whether I'm capable. I learnt to fly a helicopter because I loved the feeling of freedom. I was proud the day I passed my theory exam at 50, and ecstatic when I passed my flight test.

Now my drone is my aircraft, and that feeling is still the same. Freedom.

Five years ago, I had no expectations of what I could achieve. Now I know this: in a world where my spirit had been squashed, it took courage to choose self-trust over approval.

I no longer needed permission to take risks. Quietly, the old Amway slogan crept back in - 'If it's to be, it's up to me'.

A Fortunate Lens

"The camera is an instrument that teaches people how to see without a camera."

~ Dorothea Lange

Photography entered the silence of my pain gently. At first there was no ambition or career in it. It was a refuge and a reason to be outside, to breathe and to look outward when looking inward felt too confronting. I didn't photograph to capture perfection. Photography anchored me in the present.

Over time, something subtle but profound began to happen. It began as a tiny glimpse… a thought.

My old Instagram name needed to change. I reflected on how my life had shifted with this new love of capturing beauty, and the leap felt right. I'd be known as a_fortunate_lens. I appreciated what I saw through my lens, and I wasn't afraid to show it. It gave me a warm, slightly surprised feeling to realise I might inspire others, and show people a world they didn't have time to notice.

I started seeing resilience in trees shaped by harsh climates, and the quiet persistence of landscapes that endure the elements and expect no applause. I learnt to listen to the quiet space in nature. Nature didn't beg to be saved. It simply continued.

Without realising it, I started doing the same. In learning composition, where to stand, what to frame, and what to leave out, I learnt that what you don't include matters just as much as what you do. I learnt patience. Most of all, I learnt light doesn't erase the cracks. It enters through them.

That day on the beach, camera in hand, I thought I was searching for a masterpiece. Looking back, I was learning to trust myself again. I mattered. The things I noticed, deeply personal as they were, could shine a light for others.

That beach sunrise was the beginning of self-trust.

I didn't know it then, but this way of seeing became my language. My work. My passion. My way forward. My way back to myself. Through my lens, I wasn't escaping life. I was entering it.

Time to Shine

There was a time I believed light belonged to other people, not me, those with certainty, support, uninterrupted paths forward. I thought that if I could endure and survive, I could be around longer to spend time with my family. My mission was to keep going quietly, without expecting more.

I didn't have formal training in photography, but it was a gift I couldn't ignore. I accepted the challenge of an interview for a Master's in Photography. I prepared as best I could without really knowing what I was doing. Two days later, I had a letter of offer.

Stepping outside my comfort zone has led me onto a national stage in art, exhibiting in Melbourne and Sydney alongside nationally acclaimed artists, people from all walks of life who took a risk and followed their dreams. I took that leap too, sharing my photography and gaining recognition in regional galleries. Who would have thought I'd ever have that sort of courage?

Now the stage is set for new learning curves and new adventures. My passion is teaching others to use their creativity, whatever form it takes, and to believe they can do more than they think. What I know now is light isn't just for the unbroken.

Shine is my word. It's not about being perfect or even being fearless. It's about using fear as fuel. Shine is choosing to remain open when life's given you every reason to close. It's standing in your truth even when your voice trembles, and allowing yourself to be seen exactly as you are.

I've learnt that shining doesn't mean erasing your past. It means letting everything you've lived through shape the way you move forward. The cracks need to remain, because the light needs to get in.

Today, I stand grounded in who I am, not because the path was easy, but because I chose to keep walking. I chose to see my life as fortunate through my own lens. I allowed myself to believe, first through others, and then through myself. I once thought I needed permission to be me, to shine like the sun did that morning by the ocean. I don't need permission.

In my mind, I return to that beach, not chasing the perfect shot. Just standing where the waves are moving, where the sky changes, and where the light arrives in its own time. I set the tripod in the sand, lift the camera, and watch the first glow spill across the waterline.

The cracks are still there, but so is the light.

"The meaning of life is to find your gift. The purpose of life is to give it away."

~ Pablo Picasso

About the Author

Diane Armstrong is a Fine Art Landscape Photographer and Visual Storyteller. When behind the lens, time slows, and the noise of the world falls away. She seeks out unique encounters with wild places and untamed beauty, creating images that invite stillness, wonder, and reflection in everyday spaces.

With several regional gallery awards and the honour of national recognition, her fine art prints represent more than places; they are expressions of connection - to land, light, and spirit.

Diane's journey hasn't been easy. *In her heart lies the guiding principle "A Fortunate Lens", the place she arrived at after life changed forever.* It is both philosophy and gratitude - a reminder of the privilege of connection, of being entrusted with moments that cannot be repeated. It shapes the way she sees, transforming the ordinary into the extraordinary.

Diane's genuine aspiration lies in inspiring others, encouraging others to follow their own passions.

Website: www.dianearmstrong.com.au

Facebook: www.facebook.com/p/Diane-Armstrong-Photography

Instagram:

www.instagram.com/diane_armstrong_photography

Leanne Carter

Have you ever felt called to something you couldn't explain?

I didn't understand the pull to Uluru, I just knew I had to go.

It didn't make sense. It wasn't something that I could explain… but something deep in me kept nudging, whispering, pushing until eventually I stopped trying to reason with it and simply listened. At the time, I thought it was just a trip: a reset after the heaviness of COVID. I had no idea I was walking toward a moment that would change my life forever.

From the outside, my life looked fine, successful even, but inside, I felt stuck.

I was working in a role and environment that wasn't right for me. Deep down I knew it wasn't where I was meant to be or what I was meant to be doing, but I continued to show up each day, not because I didn't want to chase my dreams… but because fear felt louder than my dreams.

I had this vision of starting my own business, building something meaningful, creating a legacy… but every time I went to take the next step, imposter syndrome hit hard.

What if I fail?
What if I'm not good enough?
Why would anyone want to hear what I have to say?

Despite having done heaps of courses, personal development and healing, I still couldn't move forward. I kept going through the motions, but it didn't feel like purpose, it felt like survival. Like I was a hamster on a wheel, always moving but going nowhere. I couldn't see it at the time, but I wasn't just unhappy, I was dysregulated, depleted and disconnected from myself.

Looking back, the three biggest blocks I faced were:

- Self-doubt and imposter syndrome

- Hyper-independence and emotional self-protection

- Nervous system overload and survival-mode living

Beneath it all, one question kept circling:

Surely there is more to life than this.

In my personal life I had such a beautiful circle of friends, people who would've done anything for me, but I wasn't able to fully let them in. My past had made me fiercely independent and my mindset was always: *I can do this on my own and I don't need anyone's help.*

I was comfortable always being the one supporting everyone else, the one holding it all together, never asking for, or expecting, anything in return.

In a strange way, receiving help felt harder than giving it. It felt unfamiliar… like I was better off doing things on my own.

Looking back, that wasn't independence, it was survival.

And then came the moment that shifted everything…

The pull to Uluru became impossible to ignore. It wasn't planned, it wasn't practical, but something deep inside kept nudging me until I finally stopped trying to reason with it.

A friend and I booked the flights and tour… not realising we were stepping into a moment that would change my life forever. Then, right before the trip, she broke her ankle and couldn't travel, but something in me still said to go. I didn't know why, I just knew I was meant to be there, so I went anyway, alone.

The trip was magical, the beauty, the spirituality, the history, the vastness… it felt ancient and grounding in a way I still struggle to explain. Standing there, I remember feeling small in the best way, like life was bigger than the day-to-day stress I'd been carrying for so long.

The real turning point came in the most unexpected way.

While collecting firewood, I cut my leg on a native tree. I didn't think much of it at the time, just that it was an annoying little injury, but it became infected…

When I got home, things didn't feel right. The lymph nodes in my armpit were inflamed, my right breast and nipple were swollen and so painful… and then I felt it: a significant lump.

My GP suspected mastitis but sent me for an ultrasound just to be safe. That ultrasound was immediately followed by an unplanned mammogram on the same day and suddenly it no longer felt like a precaution. The biopsy was booked for first thing the next morning.

And then came the diagnosis that shattered my world:

Invasive Carcinoma (Breast cancer)

The word "cancer" landed like a bomb.

I vividly remember the day I had to tell my babies (at the time my daughter was 13 and my son was 8). The very first thing they asked me was:

"Mummy… are you going to die?"

Even though my heart was breaking, I looked them in the eyes and said, *"No. I'm kicking it to the curb."*

In that moment, nothing else mattered, not the scans or treatments or the unknown to come. All I cared about was reassuring them that I wasn't going anywhere, that I would always be here for them and that I would fight this thing with everything I had.

What followed was a whirlwind of appointments, tests, decisions to be made… and eventually, the terrifying choice to have a double mastectomy.

Whilst I was comfortable with my decision, there was one part that I didn't expect to struggle with as much as I did: the thought of waking up without my breasts… Honestly, that terrified me. It wasn't vanity, it was identity: I genuinely worried that I wouldn't feel like myself or recognise myself anymore. So, I chose immediate reconstruction (a DIEP flap), knowing it would be a bigger surgery and a harder recovery, but I needed to feel "whole" and still like me.

The surgery lasted 13 hours, but the recovery didn't go to plan and due to complications, I was back in theatre the very next day for an unplanned second surgery.

In total, it was 19 hours of surgery over two days.

Recovery was brutal. I couldn't lift my arms. I couldn't shower myself. I couldn't even go to the bathroom without needing help. For the first time in my life, I had no choice but to surrender and let people help me.

And they did.

My friends and children showed up in ways I will never forget and will always be grateful for. They created a schedule of who would do the grocery shopping, cooking, cleaning, washing my hair, changing dressings, driving me to hospital appointments and ensuring I was never alone. They held me through the most vulnerable season of my life.

Cancer stripped away my ability to do it all alone and that's where the shift began.

Because up until then, I had been living like survival was a personality trait. I was the capable one. The strong one. The one who could handle anything. I didn't just avoid asking for help, I didn't even know how. I'd built my identity around being independent, reliable and "fine," even when I wasn't.

And in the middle of recovery, I started to see something I'd never fully acknowledged before:

I hadn't been living from self-trust.
I'd been living from self-protection.

I realised how many decisions I'd been making from fear, fear of failing, being judged, getting it wrong, needing people, taking up space. And I realised that the same patterns that kept me safe in the past were now keeping me stuck.

I started noticing it everywhere: in how I overthought everything, in how my nervous system stayed on high alert, in how I pushed myself through exhaustion, in how I stayed in roles that didn't fit because it felt safer than being seen.

That was the deeper healing.

Not just recovering physically… but learning how to feel safe in my own life again.

This became the foundation for everything that followed, not just how I rebuilt myself, but how I now guide other women to rebuild their confidence, careers and sense of self from the inside out.

What I discovered was this:

Receiving isn't weakness, it's connection.

It gives others the opportunity to show up, to contribute, to feel useful and to love you out loud.

That lesson didn't just change how I healed… it changed how I lived.

After everything I'd been through, I didn't rush to reinvent myself. I chose stability, not because I was scared, but because I needed solid ground to rebuild from. I accepted a corporate role to steady myself financially and focused on completing my qualifications: a Master's in Holistic Counselling and Empowerment and a Diploma of Kinesiology.

I wasn't chasing more certificates… I was rebuilding my confidence, my identity and my sense of purpose slowly, carefully and practically, from the inside out.

This is something I now teach the women I work with:

Stability isn't always fear. Sometimes it's wisdom.

Sometimes it's the safety your nervous system needs before you take your next brave step.

Over time, something in me shifted. The version of me who used to overthink, second-guess, stay small and talk herself out of what she wanted… she wasn't running the show anymore. I started listening to my intuition, trusting myself again and making decisions from a more grounded place instead of fear.

I also became much better at receiving support, not just physically, but emotionally too. Relationships became more balanced. I learnt that letting people in doesn't make you weak… it connects you. It makes you human and that came with a deeper sense of purpose.

A trip back to my hometown, Cape Town, made it crystal clear: I was ready.

Ready to stop waiting for the "perfect time"

Ready to back myself and start building what I'd dreamt of for years.

Then life gave me another nudge.

Returning to work, I was told there was an internal restructure and redundancy was on the table. It was confronting… but it also felt like a doorway, an opportunity, like the universe was saying, *"Here. This is your moment."*

I took the leap, the one I had been too scared to take before, but it was different this time: I didn't try to do it all alone. Instead, I found a business coach and mentor and invested in support, because I finally understood something that cancer had forced me to learn:

Receiving doesn't make you weak, it's strength, it's leadership.

And that's how I now support other women, not just with strategy, but with safety. Not just with career tools, but with nervous system awareness, emotional steadiness, and deep self-trust.

Because what I've seen, in myself and in the women I work with, is that the biggest thing holding women back is rarely capability.

It's:

- the habit of second-guessing.

- The fear of being judged.

- The pressure to keep proving.

- The constant "I'll do it myself" survival strategy that looks strong on the outside... but feels exhausting on the inside.

And the cost is real.

It impacts health, relationships, confidence and identity. It keeps women in roles that don't fit anymore. It keeps them playing small in rooms they've earned their place in.

What people think they need is a better resume or more job applications.

What they truly want is deeper:

- **Clarity** — to know what direction is right for them now

- **Confidence** — to trust their skills, experience and instincts again

- **Purpose** — to do work that feels meaningful and aligned

- **Momentum** — to move forward instead of staying stuck

- **Recognition** — to be valued without over-functioning

- **Balance** — a career that fits their life, not consumes it

These desires are not superficial, they are human. They are valid. And they are possible.

This is where my work begins: **at the intersection of career clarity, nervous system safety and grounded self-leadership.**

I'm not coaching from theory. I've spent over 20 years inside corporate HR and Recruitment, reviewing thousands of resumes, sitting in interview panels and watching what really makes someone stand out. I've seen why strong, capable women get overlooked.

I work with women who are intelligent, capable and experienced, but stuck. Women who look successful on paper but privately question if they're in the right job, the right organisation, or even the right career. Women who carry a lot emotionally, mentally, professionally and over time, that pressure chips away at their confidence.

I help them do the deeper work first: rebuilding self-trust, clarity and courage.

Then we make it practical: strategy, positioning, interviews, leadership confidence, boundaries, so they can step into careers that feel aligned, sustainable and genuinely fulfilling.

The real shift happens when they stop outsourcing their worth… and start backing themselves again.

That moment changes everything.

Client Story #1:

One woman came to me feeling stuck and unfulfilled. She'd stepped down from her leadership role because she'd lost confidence in herself and imposter syndrome was loud. Together, we rebuilt her identity and leadership presence from the inside out. She became clear on her direction, started making decisions with certainty again and began targeting roles and organisations aligned with her values, not just what looked good on paper. Within weeks, she secured a role back in leadership, this time from self-trust, not survival.

Client story #2:

Another client came to me feeling overwhelmed and panicked about finding work. She'd applied for countless roles with no success and was spiralling into "maybe I'm not good enough." We worked on strengthening her self-belief, calming her nervous system response and refining her resume and interview presence so she could show up grounded and confident, not from fear. She secured a role that felt aligned and more importantly, she stopped questioning her worth every time she hit submit.

Client story #3:

I also supported a woman who was impacted by redundancy after twenty years in the same organisation. She felt devastated, lost and unsure how to compete in a job market that felt unfamiliar. She described feeling "institutionalised" and terrified of starting again. We worked through the identity hit first, then clarified her strengths, rebuilt her confidence and created a clear strategy to position her for the current market. She didn't just find a job in a new industry, she rebuilt her confidence, her identity and her future.

I share this because I know what it's like to feel stuck, know that you are meant for more but secretly wonder if you've missed your chance.

These women didn't need fixing. They needed self-trust, safety and a clear pathway forward.

Sometimes it starts with one brave decision to trust yourself and I believe every woman deserves the chance to do exactly that.

These stories are why I'm building what's next.

Right now, I'm finalising the next chapter of my work: moving beyond one-to-one coaching into group programs and leadership spaces where women can rise together.

This will be a grounded, trauma-informed group container for women who are ready to stop *surviving* their careers and start leading their lives with clarity and self-trust.

It's designed to bridge the inner and outer work:

- nervous system safety and emotional steadiness

- identity and confidence rebuilding

- practical career strategy (direction, positioning, interviews, boundaries, leadership presence)

So women don't just land a role, they become the woman who can hold it.

When I look at what I've been through, I can see it clearly: none of it was random.

Uluru. Infection. Breast pain. Diagnosis. Surgeries. Recovery. Surrender. Learning to receive.

It's like life forced me to stop, not to punish me, but to wake me up.

It showed me that I was never meant to live in survival mode, or to do life alone.

And that the quiet inner voice I kept ignoring was guiding me all along.

The pull to Uluru was the first time in a long time I truly listened to myself.

That same inner knowing guides how I live and how I lead my work.

My vision is simple:

I want women to stop abandoning themselves - In their careers, their relationships and in the way they over-function, while quietly running on empty.

To stop shrinking in rooms they've earned their place in, sacrificing their health to prove their worth, or building "successful" lives that don't feel like theirs.

Because when a woman reconnects with self-trust, everything changes.

A woman who backs herself doesn't just change jobs, she changes her family line:

Her children learn what self-worth looks like.
Her relationships become healthier and more balanced.
Her workplace benefits from regulated, emotionally mature leadership.
And future generations grow up seeing that leadership can be powerful and human.

This is the change I'm here to help lead.

I understand the external world: over 20 years inside corporate HR and Recruitment, seeing how decisions are really made and why capable women are often overlooked.

I also understand the internal world: the part rarely spoken about in boardrooms:

- Nervous system overload

- Self-doubt

- Emotional labour

- People-pleasing and perfectionism

- Survival patterns that shape how women lead, speak and show up

What I've learned is simple, but profound:

A woman doesn't need to be "fixed." She needs to feel safe enough to rise.

That's the future I'm building, intentionally.
Not another hustle story, or another "push harder, prove more" narrative.

I'm building pathways for women to rise by returning to themselves.

And I'm taking this conversation into bigger rooms, into

workplaces, leadership forums and onto stages, because too many environments still reward burnout and emotional suppression as the price of success.

I want to help shift that.

To bring forward a model of leadership where ambition and wellbeing can co-exist, where success doesn't require self-abandonment and where women don't have to harden or shrink to be taken seriously.

Because this is how impact happens.

Not through louder achievement, but through braver alignment.

If this story has stirred something in you, that's not random either, maybe it's your own inner voice asking for more: more clarity, more support, more truth, more courage to stop settling for a life that looks fine on the outside but doesn't feel right on the inside.

You don't have to navigate that alone.

If you'd like to be supported as you reconnect with your confidence, clarity and direction, I'm currently finalising my group program and will be opening registrations soon.

Or if you're a workplace or event organiser wanting to bring this conversation into your organisation, I also offer speaking and workshops focused on sustainable leadership, emotional wellbeing and self-trust at work.

Because when women rise differently, everything around them rises too.

If my story has taught me anything, it's this:

That quiet inner voice you keep ignoring. It's often the truest part of you.

And sometimes the smallest decision, to listen, is the one that changes everything.

That, to me, is what it means to be a voice of impact.

About the Author

Leanne du Toit Carter is a Career and Leadership Coach and the founder of Four Seasons Advisory & Wellbeing, supporting women to navigate career transitions with clarity, confidence and self-trust. With over 20 years' experience in corporate HR and Recruitment, she has reviewed thousands of applications, sat on interview panels and understands how hiring and leadership decisions are truly made.

Leanne holds a Master's in Holistic Counselling and Empowerment and blends practical career strategy with trauma-informed coaching to help women move forward without burning out or abandoning themselves. Her work has been recognised in the career development space, including being named one of Brisbane's Top 15 Career Coaches by Influence Digest.

Originally from Cape Town and now based in Queensland, Australia, Leanne is a mum of two who is passionate about helping women rise into careers and leadership that feel aligned, sustainable and true.

Email: leanne@fourseasonswellbeing.com.au

Instagram: www.instagram.com/fourseasonswellbeing

LinkedIn: www.linkedin.com/in/leanne-carter

Lisa Chothia

What would have to happen for you to leave your life?

I had a pretty normal childhood, well as normal as you can get moving every few years as my family were in the RAF. I never really had a life plan or any sort of calling so by my 30s I'd followed the expected route; GCSE's, A level's, degree at university without much to write home about. I had a few failed relationships but again nothing too out of the ordinary. Work had been going well, I was into my second career, having already qualified and worked as a riding instructor, and I now found myself climbing a career ladder back in London working full-time as an office manager and studying part-time. I had my own flat, a hectic social life with several groups of friends that I saw regularly. I'd worked hard to build a life for myself as a single young woman working and living in London.

It was October 2008, I was so proud of myself and where I was. I'd planned this phase of my life (working and studying) meticulously. Getting myself into a maintenance phase exercise-wise and keeping up with my group of friends who liked good food and music. To me I was ready, I was in the best shape of my life. Little did I know that my life was about to change massively but not because of my planning!

I woke up as usual to get ready for work but noticed I had the start of a rash. One of the girls in my office's day job was pregnant, so I messaged my boss with photos to say I felt okay but due to the rash, I wasn't going to come in for fear of infection. He agreed despite wanting proof that I wasn't lying (great boss!). I then phoned my GP who recommended that I take an antihistamine and "hoped I didn't live alone" er yes I did (I was very proud of my independence), he then explained if I wasn't able to breathe to call for an ambulance! I was still trying to figure out how that would work (making a phone call if you can't breathe) as I took the antihistamine and I hid in my flat as the rash spread and I felt worse, like having a cold but no snot is how I described it. The rash kept spreading, like everywhere, it totally covered me. Another call to the GP, I was unable to think straight, needing someone else to tell me what to do, they advised me to go to my nearest accident and emergency (A&E). It still took me another day to get myself together enough to leave my flat.

The first taxi took one look at me and drove off but thankfully the second one took me. I walked into the Royal London A&E, I'd barely said my name at reception and nurses were rushing to me getting me onto a stretcher, I was vaguely aware I had been slowly collapsing as they took me round to the ward. I was in and out of consciousness and every time I woke up the consultant speaking to me was older and more experienced, I fully expected an injection or a pill and to be sent home so I was confused why they weren't doing anything. I remember being admitted and moved to another ward and a kind nurse asked if I had anyone with me. I'd managed to explain I lived alone and my parents had just moved to York, I can't remember to this day if I called or text but I knew my mum eventually arrived and was allowed to see me despite it being very much after hours. Because of the rash they covered me in a gloop and my temperature spiked into the 40's. I remember asking the nurse, surely I wasn't the only one that had noticed a correlation between gloop and temperature? She checked the notes and they stopped. I was aware that I had no control of my body as a nurse tried to take blood and I started shaking, she told me to keep still and I remember rolling my eyes and saying if I could I would, she then realised it was my whole body convulsing. Again I was in and out of consciousness. They'd been running tests and they were all getting worse. I remember a queue of white coats prodding and poking me, intrusive personal questions and needles so many needles and drips. I was studying nutrition so I refused to eat the hospital food, my mum advocated for me. I remember waking up as she was having a full-blown row with the senior ward nurse.

They were worried about my organs, my liver especially. Still the rash persisted and still they didn't know what it was. I ate simple food my mum brought from my flat; porridge, humus and crackers and beetroot soup. Slowly I turned a corner and my tests started to improve. I remember my skin peeled like snakes shed theirs and still the white coats had no answers, no label.

Ultimately I was in hospital for about 3 or 4 weeks. I went from every department in the hospital wanting to be involved to hardly seeing anyone in a day. I was discharged not knowing if it would happen again, the sheet of paper said toxic erythema which means toxic red skin and I've since been told that when they give you the Latin it often means they don't know. I was shocked, stunned that none of the various consultants I saw were interested in finding out the what, the why, the how. These men (and they were all men) were supposed to be the best of the best but had dropped me like a hot coal the minute I started getting better. Didn't they even want to know how I'd got better, what was the magic sauce?! How do I stop it happening again? I asked them, er just hope it doesn't was the only answer I got. The haematologist was the most intrigued, he'd never been able to speak to someone who had such bad blood readings as I should have died!

Later I learned that as well as the rash my whole body had swollen which included my internal organs. I took so long to leave my flat as I hadn't recognised the person looking back at me in the mirror. My swollen brain impacting my thought processes. Most likely the taxi had driven off as he was scared I had some infectious disease, to him I probably looked like the elephant woman. I've seen the shows on TV where people arrive in hospital and the medical staff are concerned if they're going to live. I didn't expect that to be me. I was admitted tachycardic (with an irregular heartbeat) and they were still scratching their heads. My mum had been allowed to see me as they had not expected me to live much longer, my body was shutting down and my vital signs showed I was dying. She can probably write her own chapter on the worst five hours of her life getting from York to London and not recognising her own child, as she had walked past me on the ward until the nurse helped her. The human body doesn't have to go much above 40 degrees centigrade before brain damage occurs. If I hadn't managed to advocate for myself and stop them covering me in gloop I would have died before my mum had a chance to get there.

You'd think I would be happy to have been alive and I was but I flipped between extremes. From let's do, eat, drink see everything as who knows if it will happen again and this time I'll die, to overcautious I can't possibly eat that I can't do that.

I was plagued by the question what can I do with the second chance I've been given how could I make sure it didn't happen? I wanted answers and spent a huge amount of time and energy seeing any and all specialists both in orthodox and complementary medicine. No one could tell me, I should just "be glad to be alive".

By 2010 I was running on fumes. I didn't know what had happened to me, couldn't prevent it and now I was too tired and fatigued to do anything. It felt like everything I'd been trying to build was now out of control and spun the wrong way. I was overwhelmed. I felt guilty and depressed, sometimes wishing I'd not survived and never woken up that day in hospital.

The three years of illness and searching for answers had taken it's toll. In fact as soon as I was in that hospital those I'd thought were close friends vanished. If I couldn't go out and party like we used to we had nothing in common apparently. The great life I thought I had with an extensive friendship group disappeared overnight and I was too exhausted, too tired to even try and stop it. No one understood how I felt, often not even me. My once super close relationship with my parents was now incredibly strained. My mum was struggling with health issues (in hindsight mainly brought on by worry about me and my erratic behaviour) but I was too caught up in trying to get through each day at work, trying to single-handedly fire-fight my own life.

Every which way I looked I couldn't see how I could survive if I stayed in London, the city was draining, trying to keep my life going was draining. I was overwhelmed, struggling to go to work every day. I'd now been labelled with Chronic Fatigue, a seemingly catch all answer when no one could understand why all the tests came back low to normal but the symptoms I had were crucifying me. I became all too aware that something was going to give, would it be me, would I end up in hospital again, would it be the end this time?

I sat down one night and tried to break it down on a piece of paper. It had to be basic as I was now struggling to read or write anything. I can remember crying as I wrote down the question 'What is going to give?' and that's when my brain kicked in and with a strange clarity said "NO it's not gonna be me!" and I became hyper focused.

The logic in my brain said if London held nothing but pain I had to leave. It was a big scary decision. Not just moving flat, this was leaving everything I'd built, leaving my independence, resigning from my career and going to the unknown. The last place I remembered feeling happy was in North Yorkshire and it just so happened that's where my parents had moved to. The plan formulated. Move north and take the pressure off, move north and rekindle the relationship with my parents. If they weren't keen I could suggest I was doing it to look after Mum to give Dad a break.

Suddenly everything became simple action steps; first call my Dad to see if I could move home. I fully expected him to say no after how things were but they were fully supportive. The goal was set; move to my parents in Yorkshire, leave the life that was draining me and put myself back in control, simple right?! Well anyone that has ever moved knows its one of the most stressful events in your life and here I was about to move a few hundred miles, to an area where I knew no one, had no job, nothing but my parents and I wouldn't really know how they'd be until I got there.

The hyperfocus forced me to take one day one activity at a time and slowly everything fell into place. I left my job, my flat was packed up and rented out. I drove a white van from London to York with my entire life in it praying it was the right thing to do but at the same time knowing it was. Once I got home I could rest and let the healing begin. I had to make peace with the fact that I would probably never know what the illness or virus was that had happened or if it would happen again, make peace with not having a career, make peace with the stigma of having failed at living in London…bang there I was 37 living with my parents with no job and not knowing if I could ever work again.

That often hit hard and I would question what my life was, why my life was like this but I kept reminding myself to keep the action simple, control the parts I could.

There were some very dark moments. A bonus I discovered to having the chronic fatigue label was access to group counselling therapy and because I was unemployed it gave me a reduced rate. I eventually signed up to claim job seekers, a process made simple by the lady at the job centre who ticked some boxes which meant I didn't have to turn up in person each week, which was extremely helpful as we lived in a country village and I couldn't afford a car. Everything had been stripped from me, my health, my career, my friends, my independence and yet I still felt like a fraud in the therapy sessions.

I was still searching for the silver bullet that would give me my life back, give me 'a' life back. It started with slowly being able to read. I'd always been interested in human behaviours and development so I immersed myself in self-help books, looking for any clue, any sign, any 'thing' that I could apply to myself, that I was able to do.

One recommended a gratitude journal. Write down three things each day that I was grateful for. They can be the smallest of things but write at least three. I kept a little book by my bed, I made a deal with myself to do it each night. It was hard at first but gradually I started noticing more things throughout the day (cloud formations, my eyebrows, a song on the radio) and started looking forward to writing them down. Another exercise was to allow the negative voices to shout in my head but instead of entertaining them and following them along the path of "I'm 37, unemployed, no independence, no prospects…" say thank you that's not useful to me now and let them go quickly. That was tough, I'd become so good at beating myself up, but I persevered. The voices were something **I** was truly in control of as they were in **my** head, and slowly I found that not only could I banish them away I could actually switch the negative to a positive, I moved from 'why me?' to 'try me!'.

Deep down I realised that from the moment I was ill I'd already known how lucky I was. That even when I felt totally alone and powerless against a life-threatening mystery illness, I could still harness my internal power and clarity to have some influence on my life. I used what I knew about tackling change; to keep things simple, focus on only what is within the gift of your control. At the time you might not realise what you are capable of controlling. For example I firmly believe to this day that the food choices I made in hospital are what kept me alive and ultimately those early life experiences enabled me to make the decision to save my own life by leaving one chapter of it behind.

A new focus began for me, how could I use these seemingly innate skills to help others. In 2014 I (finally) had the courage to start my own nutritional therapy business. I helped individuals on a 1:1 basis navigate some of the biggest changes in their lives. My clients ranged from those wanting to improve their relationship with food, fellow chronic fatigue sufferers to those the orthodox medical profession had given up on. Much of this work has by definition been genuinely holistic and reached far beyond pure nutritional therapy. Then I was invited to deliver wellbeing workshops to corporates, our work took us all over the country. Seeing the lightbulbs go off when speaking to large groups of people was fantastic and working alongside other nutritional therapists enabled us to share and grow our skills.

Slowly step by step I've improved my own health, developed a new relationship with my parents, a new career, a new friendship group and I have my own home and life. It's not been straightforward and there has definitely been more than one twist in the road, particularly when navigating it all with chronic fatigue and recently having found out I'm autistic (all for another part of my story) but reminding myself of what I have overcome and what is within my control has been key.

I now use my life experience and skills in training, development and coaching to help organisations and individuals experiencing, planning, and needing change to work through difficult decisions and situations. I currently work mainly with a corporate organisation as a 'Change Optimisation Consultant'. I've completed qualifications in change and in coaching but at the end of the day I believe it is the experiences we've had, often the ones that might feel insignificant at the time, that enable us to draw from within and find the right strategy. The term 'transferable skills' is very popular now and that's certainly been the case with me. Many think the event, the sudden mystery illness, the near-death experience was the thing to overcome but I know and hopefully you can now also see, that was just the catalyst, the push I needed to make the life changing decision to walk (or drive a white van) away and allow that life to die so that I could start really living.

About the Author

Lisa Chothia is a change specialist living in Northern England with her rescue dog and partner – having recently found her soulmate.

As a qualified Change Management and NLP Practitioner alongside her work as a change consultant, Lisa is committed to supporting people through some of life's most challenging transitions. Her lived experience and recent autism diagnosis shapes the compassionate, down-to-earth way she works with others, helping them reconnect with their strengths, rebuild confidence and find a sense of direction when things feel uncertain.

Believing change happens when genuinely seen and supported, for over 30 years she has had a passion for developing others. Qualifying as a BHS riding instructor in her twenties and as Nutritional therapist in her thirties where she gained the Patrick Holford award for Success in the Face of Adversity.

Lisa loves travel, walks with her dog, sharing great food with her partner and fantasy books.

Instagram: www.instagram.com/cfs_hub
LinkedIn: www.linkedin.com/in/lisachothia

Karen Dawn

Surviving to Soaring – The Woman
I Became

There comes a time in every woman's life when she must stop waiting to be rescued—by her past, her family, her circumstances—and finally rise for herself.

Not for applause.
Not for permission.
But because the weight of staying silent, small, and stuck has become heavier than the fear of the unknown.

For me, that moment didn't arrive with fireworks or some blinding moment of clarity. It crept in slowly—through the cracks of my spirit, through the moments of quiet devastation that no one else saw. It wasn't loud. It wasn't dramatic. It was subtle and soul-shattering: the kind of exhaustion that comes from being chronically unseen. The kind of ache that builds after years of being the one who holds everyone else together, while falling apart in silence.

I had grown used to being misunderstood. Labelled. Misjudged. Dismissed as "too emotional." Told I was overreacting. Branded the difficult one. The troublemaker. The one who felt too deeply and spoke too boldly. But those labels weren't true — they were projections. And over time, I began to realise they weren't mine to carry.

Still, the damage had already been done. Years of emotional invalidation had slowly eroded my sense of self. I had internalised those voices, confused their opinions with my worth. Pain doesn't always scream—it can whisper quietly in the background of your life, so consistently that you forget what it feels like to live without it. You start thinking pain is your baseline. That struggle is your default.

I grew up carrying traumas I didn't have the language to explain—let alone the support to process. As a young girl, I experienced things no child should ever have to endure. I was kidnapped—ripped away from safety in a way that fractures the nervous system and rewires your very sense of what's safe in the world. Then, not long after, two men broke into my bedroom through the window, louvre by louvre, like a horror story unfolding in slow motion. They didn't just steal my peace—they stole the innocence and safety every child deserves to have unquestioned.

And still… There was no help.
No counselling.

No soft place to land.

No one saying "What happened to you matters."

Just silence. Deafening, just-get-on-with-it, silence.

So I learned to do what so many women learn to do far too young: I put on a brave face, pretended I was fine, and survived.

Because I didn't feel like I had a choice.

And years later, that unhealed pain shaped the life I unconsciously walked into. I found myself in a marriage defined by control, manipulation, and emotional abuse. Twenty-three years of walking on eggshells. Twenty-three years of eroded self-worth, devastating betrayal, repeated lying and cheating, unhinged gaslighting, and pure survival mode.

I gave everything I had - my love, my loyalty, my energy - and it still wasn't enough.

Because in relationships rooted in power imbalance, nothing you give will ever fill what's broken in them.

When I finally left, people said I was brave. And yes - I was! But what they didn't see was that leaving was only the beginning of the battle.

What came after was equally - if not more - painful.

I endured years of relentless stalking and threats, while he weaponised my childhood trauma and fears.

I was dealt a double blow with the crushing grief of family estrangement. The betrayal of people I once trusted with my heart.

Then came the traumatic brain injury—sudden, devastating, and life-altering.
I was placed on life support, in a coma, with my children not knowing whether I would live or die.

When I finally woke, nothing felt the same. My body, my brain, my sense of identity—everything had changed.

I had to relearn how to speak, to walk, to function in a world that no longer felt familiar.

Years of rehabilitation, therapy, and specialist appointments followed. I was physically alive, but emotionally fractured and disoriented.

Even the simplest tasks became overwhelming mountains. I questioned if I would ever feel whole again—mentally, emotionally, or spiritually.

But even then, in the silence of that slow, painful recovery… something inside me whispered: **"There is more for you than this."**

At first, I ignored it. Doubted it. Thought maybe that voice was just wishful thinking. But eventually, the whisper became a flame. And the flame became a fire.

And that fire? It burned away everything I thought I was supposed to be.

Since sharing my story in *Voices of Impact Volume 2*, my life hasn't just continued —it has **transformed**.

Not because the pain magically disappeared. Not because life suddenly became easy. But because *I* became different.

I got clearer.
I got stronger.
I stopped seeking approval in the wrong places.
I started anchoring into the truth—my truth.

I stopped waiting to be chosen and started choosing myself.

I let go of the "good girl" conditioning. I shed the roles I had played for decades—caretaker, fixer, people-pleaser, peacekeeper.

I no longer needed to perform to be worthy. I started becoming the woman I was always meant to be.

And who is the woman I became through all of this?

She is deeply grounded in her own power.
She no longer seeks external validation— she started living her truth.

And she is fiercely committed to helping other women do the same.

But make no mistake— this transformation didn't come from

books or theories. It came from doing the real work—first on myself, and then with others.

It came from feeling everything I had spent years avoiding. From facing the hardest truths. From sitting with my pain until it told me what it came to teach me. From rewriting the stories I had unknowingly inherited and reclaiming the parts of myself I once buried to keep the peace.

For years, I sat across from counsellors and psychiatrists, hoping that if I could just *talk* enough, maybe something would finally shift. I shared my pain. I told my story. I unpacked childhood trauma, abuse, betrayal, emotional neglect, and every pattern I could identify. I left each session mentally exhausted but no closer to peace. It was like I was circling a wound without ever touching its centre. I kept waiting for the moment I would feel relief, release, resolution—but it never came.

What I came to realise is this: **talking about the pain isn't the same as healing it.**

I had become fluent in my trauma. I could articulate every chapter of my suffering. But knowledge alone wasn't enough to set me free. I was surviving—but I wasn't *soaring*. The deeper layers—the subconscious beliefs, suppressed emotions, and inherited patterns—were still running the show behind the scenes. No matter how many sessions I attended, no matter how "self-aware" I became, I was still stuck.

Then, everything changed.

I began training in **TimeLine Therapy®**, not yet knowing that this modality would become the key that unlocked a door I didn't even know existed.

During the practical, hands-on component of my practitioner training, I experienced a breakthrough that shifted something at the deepest core of my being. It was unlike anything I had ever felt.

In that session, I accessed a part of myself I hadn't touched in decades—a place buried beneath logic and language. A place that didn't need to *explain* the pain, but simply needed to *feel it*, move through it, and release it. And in that space, I did something I never thought possible: **I let it go.** I released emotional weight I didn't even realise I was still carrying.

No reliving. No retraumatising.

Something in me had shifted—not just mentally, but emotionally, spiritually, energetically. I felt lighter. Clearer. More peaceful than I had ever experienced through years of traditional therapy. I remember thinking, *"So this is what healing feels like."*

That moment was more than a breakthrough—it was a **Sacred Awakening**.

And it was the catalyst for everything that followed.

From that day forward, I couldn't ignore the knowing in my

bones: *this* is what I'm meant to do. Not just heal myself—but become a guide for other women who are stuck in the same cycles. Women who are brilliant, capable, intuitive, and deeply wounded. Women who have done "all the right things" and still feel like something's missing. Women who are emotionally exhausted from surviving and are desperate for something deeper.

I didn't just want to help—**I wanted to create real, lasting change. I wanted women to truly heal. I wanted to offer something that genuinely transforms lives.**

So I became a certified **Women's Life Coach, Root Cause Therapist**, and **TimeLine Therapy® Practitioner** not for prestige or letters behind my name, but because I wanted the real tools. The tools that actually *work*. Tools that go beyond mindset and really reach the *source*—the subconscious mind, the emotional body, the nervous system, and the soul.

These modalities became the foundation of my practice. They allowed me to guide women not just through their stories, but beyond them—into healing, integration, and self-reclamation.

I stopped trying to "fix" women, and instead helped them *remember* who they were before the world told them they were too much, too sensitive, too broken.

Because I know now what I didn't know then:
You don't have to carry your pain forever.

You don't have to stay stuck in the loop of your past.

Healing is not only possible—it is *inevitable* when you access the right keys.

And for me, TimeLine Therapy® was one of those keys. It was the door that opened my true inner power.

And once I walked through it, there was no turning back.

From my own healing came the birth of something deeply sacred—my signature coaching program: **Phoenix Woman Rising**.

This isn't just a program.

It's not just a mindset workshop or another surface-level course.

Phoenix Woman Rising is a reclamation.

An Awakening.

A return to the woman you were before the world asked you to shrink, silence, or settle.

It was born from my lived experience—from the ache of surviving without thriving, and from the breakthroughs that finally brought me home to myself. I created this 16-week journey for women who are done with self-help Band-Aids, who've tried all the books, the quotes, the meditations, the journaling—but still feel stuck in an emotional loop they can't quite name or escape.

It's for the woman who is coping on the outside but collapsing on the inside.

The woman who smiles while suppressing tears.

The woman who gives everything to everyone else but can't hear her own voice anymore.

Phoenix Woman Rising is where she begins to come back to life.

The journey begins with the start of a deep soul excavation. Together, we trace her story, illuminate the patterns that continue to repeat, and gently name the pain she's been carrying—often in silence. We look at where her survival strategies were born, where her trust was broken, and what she's still holding that was never meant for her in the first place.

Then, we begin the work.

And when I say "the work," I don't mean talking in circles or simply venting emotions. I mean deep, structured, intentional transformation—layer by layer, belief by belief, wound by wound.

We **Release suppressed emotions** that have been living in the body, often for decades.

We **Clear inherited trauma** passed down through generations, unconsciously shaping her choices.

We **Interrupt and rewire subconscious programs** that have kept her repeating the same patterns in relationships, work, self-worth, and identity.

We use **Root Cause Therapy, Neuro-Linguistic Programming (NLP)**, and **TimeLine Therapy®** to shift her not just intellectually, but emotionally, somatically, and energetically. These aren't tools for "managing symptoms"—they're methods for finally getting to the root and healing it from the inside out.

Because I don't just coach—I hold sacred, intuitive, non-judgmental space for women to show up fully. To speak the unspeakable. To cry without apologising. To let their guard down and say, "This is what I've been through," and be met with love—not shame.

In that space, I've witnessed true alchemy.

I've sat with women as they uncovered grief they didn't even know they had permission to feel.

I've walked with women who hadn't felt safe in their own skin for decades.

I've guided women who had silenced their voice for so long that they forgot what it sounded like.

And one by one, they remembered.

They remembered their worth.
Their voice.
Their power.

Women who came to me feeling broken walk away not as a "new" version of themselves, but as the *true* version. The version that was always there, buried beneath years of guilt, grief, and conditioning.

Phoenix Woman Rising is where SHE rises! And once she rises, she never forgets who she is again.

Real Women. Real Healing.

Every woman I've worked with carries her own story, her own wounds. But the common thread is always this: she's exhausted from *surviving*. And she's ready to *soar*.

One of the most radical, life-changing shifts in my personal journey has been letting go of the deeply ingrained need to please others.

For most of my life, I was the woman who tried to be easy—easy to love, easy to be around, easy to manage. I softened my voice so others wouldn't feel threatened. I diluted my opinions so no one would feel uncomfortable. I twisted myself into a version that made other people feel safe—even when it left me feeling invisible.

I learned early on that approval often came at the cost of authenticity. That being accepted sometimes meant being silent. That if I made things easier for everyone else, maybe—just maybe—I'd be worthy of love.

So I shaped myself on those beliefs.

I over-delivered. I over-explained. I apologised for simply

existing with emotions, needs, and boundaries. I tried to be everything for everyone—except for myself.

But over time, the cost became unbearable.

Because **people-pleasing is self-abandonment in disguise**.

And no amount of external validation can fill the void that forms when you chronically betray your own soul.

It left me feeling hollow.
Disconnected from my own truth.
Resentful of the very people I was trying so hard to please.
And exhausted—so deeply exhausted from living a life that didn't feel like mine.

The mask was heavy. The performance, unsustainable.

Eventually, I started to see the patterns. The way I had outsourced my worth to other people's comfort. The way I tiptoed around conflict to keep the peace—when really, I was sacrificing my own. The way I shrank myself in rooms where I was meant to grow.

So I made a different choice.

Today, I choose authenticity over approval.

Even when it's uncomfortable.
Even when it means I disappoint people who preferred the quiet, compliant version of me.

Even when my truth disrupts the illusion they've clung to.

Because I will no longer betray myself to keep someone else comfortable.

I no longer dim my light to fit into spaces that were never built to hold the fullness of me.

I no longer contort myself into someone else's expectations just to avoid rejection.

I no longer explain my worth to those who are committed to misunderstanding me.

I don't apologise for being emotional, intuitive, powerful, or passionate.

I am not here to be judged by others — I am here to be *true to myself*.

I am whole.

I am healing.

And I am no longer afraid to take up space—not with arrogance, but with *unapologetic ownership* of who I am.

Because every time a woman stops performing and starts embodying her truth, she gives other women permission to do the same.

And that is a ripple effect I'm proud to be part of.

There's a story we're sold about midlife—that it's a crisis. That everything starts to slow down. That our dreams fade into the background and we should just settle.

I call BS. Midlife is not a crisis. It's a *clarifier*. When I turned 40, it was like blinkers were lifted from my eyes.

It's the moment when the noise falls away, and what's true rises to the surface. It's when we stop tolerating the things we once called "normal." It's when we feel the ache for something more — not because we're broken, but because we're *awakening*.

This work became my calling – the thing that lights me up from the inside out.

Since becoming a full-time coach, I've had the honour of guiding hundreds of women through deep emotional healing. Each story reminds me of why this work matters.

I now work exclusively with women who are ready to let go of the emotional baggage that's been weighing them down.

Women in their 40s, 50s, and beyond who are done pretending.
Done settling.
Done shrinking.

These women are not in crisis.
They are standing on the edge of their transformation.

And I get to walk beside them as they rise.

What I do now is more than coaching — it's sacred leadership.

It's listening between the lines.
It's honouring trauma with tenderness.
It's calling forward the truth in women who've been silenced for too long.

I don't position myself as someone "above" my clients. I walk beside them, hand in hand, soul to soul.

Because I *am* them, I've sat in the darkness. I've doubted my worth. I've wept on the bathroom floor. And I've rebuilt myself piece by piece.

That's why I can hold the space I do. Because I've lived it. And because I know how to *hold you while you rise*.

If you're reading this and feel like I am telling your story,

That's a *breakthrough*.

Your discomfort is not your enemy—it's your invitation.
Your grief is not weakness—it's the proof that you still care, still hope, still long for more.

The woman inside you—the one you've quieted, dismissed, or ignored—is still there.

She's not gone. She's just waiting.

Waiting for you to say, "No more."
Waiting for you to come back to her.
Waiting for you to *choose yourself*.

Let this chapter be your permission slip.

To stop shrinking.
To stop apologising.
To stop just surviving.

And to start becoming the woman you were always meant to be.

I don't measure my success in followers, titles, or income.

I measure it in the women who now sleep peacefully at night.

In the mothers who no longer pass their pain down to their daughters.

In the women who finally look in the mirror and say, "I love her."

This is my legacy.

One woman at a time.

Are YOU Ready to Rise with me?

Love & Light,

Karen Dawn xx
Women's Life Coach & Root Cause Therapist

Heal Your Past, Rise Strong ~ YOU ARE WORTHY

About the Author

Karen Dawn is a Women's Life Coach, Root Cause Therapist, and Founder of *Phoenix Woman Rising*—a transformational coaching program supporting women to heal deeply, rise strong, and reclaim their self-worth. Drawing from her own lived experiences and profound personal breakthroughs, Karen specialises in subconscious healing and emotional recovery for women navigating midlife awakening, identity shifts, and the desire for deeper purpose and peace.

Through her trauma-informed, heart-centred approach, she has helped hundreds of women release long-held emotional pain, dismantle limiting beliefs, silence their inner critic, and reconnect with their innate strength and worthiness. Karen is known for creating a safe, compassionate, and empowering space where real, lasting change can occur—beyond just coping, beyond just survival.

Her work is guided by one core Mantra: **Heal Your Past, Rise Strong ~ YOU ARE WORTHY.**

Facebook: www.facebook.com/KarenDawnCoaching

Explore her transformational Signature Coaching Program *Phoenix Woman Rising,* and access Free Resources at: www.karendawncoaching.com

Or Join the Community:

www.facebook.com/groups/perfectlyimperfectwomen

Robyn Edtmaier

I stopped weighing myself because I couldn't bear to know the truth anymore.

My body was over 100 kilograms, my mind was exhausted, and every morning I woke up already disappointed in myself.

I felt sick, heavy and defeated. Not just in my body, but in my mind and my heart. Before my feet even hit the floor, I was already beating myself up for what I'd eaten the night before.

More often than not, I woke up feeling sick. The whole of my insides would feel crampy, sore and just horrible. I don't know how many times I texted my boss saying that I felt sick and wasn't coming into work. It felt like I had PMT every morning. I didn't want to move at all. I got out of bed to go to the bathroom but quickly went back to bed straight away. This continued for a very long time. I didn't want to get up. I wanted to go back to sleep and escape the nightmare of living.

I had no motivation to do anything. I didn't want to have breakfast because I felt so awful. The only thing that motivated me to get up was the thought of having a cup of coffee.

I struggled with movement of any kind because that would be doing something. Doing housework felt very hard. I would make one bed at a time because I felt so tired afterwards. I tried all sorts of strategies to motivate myself to DO things. I wrote lists, I watched cleaning and decluttering YouTube videos galore. I tried all kinds of new systems but quickly ran out of steam after creating all the new systems and actually ended up doing very little.

If someone was coming over, I would panic clean and shove all of the clutter in the spare room. I filled up boxes of clutter because I wasn't able to make decisions and deferred those decisions by throwing them in the spare room. The spare room became a dumping ground. The boxes became boxes of doom because I never got around to tackling them and making decisions about what could go.

I'd spend most of the day thinking about what I was going to eat. I ate to feel better. I ate because I was tired, because I'd just got home, because it was time, because I was bored, because the TV was on. I 'grazed' all day long. I had forgotten what it felt like to feel truly hungry. I only ever felt cravings. All through the day I'd ask myself "What do I feel like eating now?"

My inner thoughts were so negative and I truly thought I was the only person in the whole world who felt this way. I woke up beating myself up for having eaten food that I knew I didn't need yet again. What was even worse was sometimes I'd wake up realising that I'd eaten treats that I'd put away for my family. I felt incredibly guilty and ashamed of myself.

I wanted to exercise to get rid of the effect of the food that I'd eaten. I used to ask myself all the time, "What is wrong with me?"

I told myself I was happy. I had my baby and I took unpaid family leave for as long as I could. I enjoyed staying home and I was ready to stay home and be a Mum. However, I just kept putting on more weight. I had terrible adult acne. I would get surface level acne, and then really deep cystic acne. It seemed like I had acne for most of my life. I tried everything to get rid of it but nothing worked.

I hated photos being taken of me. I took a lot of photos and videos as a Mum. My husband didn't take photos, so I did. That meant that because I was the one behind the camera, I didn't have to be in the photos/videos. As a consequence, there are not many photos of me during this time. Sadly, I have very few photos of me with my family.

When someone did take a photo of me at a family gathering I would try to hide behind someone, especially the kids. When I saw someone taking a photo of the kids I would move away, so that they didn't get me in the frame.

I didn't want to go out. I didn't want to be seen. If I had to go out with my husband to a social occasion it felt like a nightmare trying to find something to wear that I was happy to be seen in. I wore a lot of big, loose tunic tops.

I hated going shopping, especially clothes shopping. I didn't want to be seen and I didn't want to see myself. It was so confronting trying clothes on in front of the mirror in the changing rooms. I only ever bought clothes from the plus section of big department stores. I would trail around the department and grab a big selection of clothes to try on and buy anything that fitted.

I loved being a Mum but I was desperately unhappy with my body and myself.

My relationship to myself was incredibly negative. I was really down on myself. I was my own worst critic. I put myself down in front of others first, convinced it would hurt less if I said it before they did.

I thought I was happy, or at least that was the story I told myself.

"I am content. I am safe and secure. I get to stay home and look after my family. I have a lovely home. I have everything I need. What more do I want?"

But I was deeply depressed. It didn't really hit me until I met a person who filled me with inspiration. She had followed her dreams overseas. She was full of determination and focus whereas I had been floating along in my life. It made me think, "Is this all there is to my life?"

It stopped me in my tracks. It became the catalyst for me to change.

I began to ask myself, "Am I happy, really? What else is out there for me?"

Like many women I know, I'd wanted to lose weight for a very long time.

I'd met a personal trainer who'd moved to our town with her children. I remember when I first met her at our local playgroup. She had the most gorgeous handbag and had brought a batch of freshly baked scones to share with us.

I began to train with her and set some real goals for the first time in my life. She began a fitness class in our town and I started going to that too.

I started to get back into exercise in other ways. I joined some local ladies to have a social hit of tennis once a week. I went to yoga once a week. I discovered there were dancing classes for adults with my daughter's dance school and I began jazz and tap. I made friends with a lady there and we started walking regularly. She was into exercise and she had her own home gym. I introduced her to my personal trainer and they became close friends. They both inspired me and helped me a lot.

Then my personal trainer decided to run a challenge. I lost 10 kg in one challenge and 10kg in another. But I wasn't really focused on what I was eating and drinking. The weight I lost started to come back because I hadn't changed what I was eating. My trainer suggested that I cut out carbs after 4pm but that seemed impossible.

I said "I think I'm addicted to carbs" and she said "Aren't we all?"

Then, my daughter's tennis coach offered to coach the ladies in our mid-week social tennis group. Since I'd had tennis lessons as a child and had played junior tennis, my hand shot up. I couldn't believe we had this opportunity in our little town!

One of my dreams at the time was to play in the adult competition on a Saturday afternoon but I didn't want to get all hot and bothered and red in the face when I played.

Then one beautiful morning I was at the tennis club for a tennis lesson with our Wednesday morning social ladies. The courts had been newly installed and were a vivid, startling bright blue. Even the skies were blue and there was not a cloud in the sky. It was an absolutely perfect day for tennis.

I was in the clubhouse and I overheard one of the ladies say to our coach that she needed to lose weight. The coach said, "No, you don't."

But in my head I said "No, but **I do!**"

This whole exchange took on a huge significance. It suddenly galvanised me. Everything I wanted suddenly became extraordinarily clear. It was as if this coach existed just for me at that moment to say these words.

I didn't realise it then, but this moment would become a line in the sand.

From that moment on, I focused on my nutrition like it was my job. I continued to exercise, doing strength training, playing tennis, running and dancing.

I had a goal, but I didn't believe I could ever reach it because I never had before. I didn't really set a time limit because I didn't believe I could reach the goal.

I measured absolutely everything I could. I monitored my progress and became so excited losing even the smallest amount, be it on the scale or my tape measure.

I concentrated on eating the best way I knew without starving myself. I learned to eat enough by calculating how many calories my Basal Metabolic Rate was. This was a big realisation for me and made a huge difference. But the calorie deficit was the reason I lost weight.

I ate mostly what I wanted. I didn't ever feel hungry. I'd made a big switch from grazing all day long and being a slave to cravings to someone eating well-balanced meals and I have never gone back.

I wouldn't say I was obsessed, but I was very intentional about what I was eating every day.

I started to feel like doing things again. My motivation began to increase. I listened to Louise Hay's affirmations for months and my self-talk began to change. I listened to Hal Elrod's book *The Miracle Morning* because I decided I wanted to get up earlier. I went to bed early and wrote on my laptop. I started journaling, meditating and reading first thing in the morning.

I lost 33kg in 6 months.

At first, I couldn't believe it. I was over the moon! I was ecstatically happy. Shopping for clothes became my new hobby. I got to play tennis with the senior team on Saturday afternoons. Not only did I look good, I felt good and I didn't get all hot and bothered and red in the face when I played. My adult acne finally cleared up for good!

I adored dancing. Getting dressed up and being on stage in sequinned costumes was another dream come true, especially once I'd lost all of the weight. However, not only had I lost weight, I had muscle definition!

I wanted to tell everyone how I'd done it, but something stopped me. Who was I to talk about weight loss?

So, I studied and became a Personal Trainer myself. I loved doing strength training and I absolutely love learning. All of the knowledge I had from my High School Biology, Physics and

Chemistry classes suddenly became valuable again!

By that time, my trainer had moved and my new friend had taken over her fitness class. After some time, she became ill and to help her out, I began running the strength training part of the class. Eventually, I ran the whole class as she became too ill to continue.

I still run that same class to this day, although, since Covid, I've been running it online.

There were so many benefits to having a body transformed. Not only was I at my ideal body weight, I was also at my strongest and fittest that I'd ever been.

I loved feeling strong and I could do more in my life without feeling exhausted. I could wash and dry all of the bed linen AND make all the beds, all in one day!

I remember the day when we bought a new mattress. We had to pull the old mattress out of the house and I remember feeling how easy it was because I was so strong and fit. It really made a huge difference in my life.

My zest for life exploded! We were invited to a wedding on Hamilton Island and my husband said we couldn't afford to go. I told him that we had to go because it was his cousin and weddings are so special. (I definitely didn't want to miss out on this!)

I had a lot of fun shopping for new outfits that I could wear to the wedding. I bought two cobalt blue dresses that made me look and feel fabulous. I took Mum with me and I remember buying one of those dresses with her. I wore that dress many times.

I started taking photos of myself because I loved how my face and body looked. I enjoyed being in photos and couldn't wait to see the results. What a difference!

Now I feel strong, fit and healthy within my body. I exercise regularly. That wasn't always the case.

Afterwards, I found out that there is such a thing as processed food addiction. Bit by bit, I gave up sugar, flour, caffeine and alcohol. The brain fog lifted and my prefrontal cortex began to work properly again. The difference was like night and day. I felt absolutely amazing all over again. My capacity to achieve new goals skyrocketed.

Women started to ask if I could help them to lose weight. I began working with small groups and also coached women individually.

It has been such a delight to be able to help others to get moving again and start to lose weight. It really fills my heart with joy when they share their successes with me.

Here is what some of the women I've worked with shared.

Susan joined my weight loss group. She lost the weight that she wanted, putting it down to my positive and helpful suggestions.

"I have lost weight and have learnt more about my body. I have lost 4kg and feel way more comfortable in my jeans. I enjoyed doing it alongside others which gave me support and recognition of effort. Definitely take up the challenge, the support and safe environment gave me purpose and persistence. Robyn has been very supportive, informative and always present. Her influence was the reason I succeeded." Susan

Karen did 6 weeks of coaching with me and lost 3kg in 3 weeks. Not only that, she has implemented so many new healthy habits it's inspiring! She has been walking 6 days a week and has started lifting weights! She is drinking water, tracking her nutrition and exercise and checking in with me daily. She has zero alcohol at recent events (3 birthday parties). She has also noticed that with the changes she has made in her nutrition, she is feeling satisfied and is no longer hungry all the time.

"Got my scales battery replaced! I'm down 5.7kg since we started and 10kg since Xmas. OMG I could not dream that I could have such great results." Karen

I began to connect with women from all over the world.

Tina worked with me for 4 weeks.

"Before I started with Robyn I was feeling kind of stuck and really unmotivated and not able to make time for exercise. Now I feel like I'm starting to get a rhythm.

Robyn did daily accountability with me for my calorie counting which

was extremely helpful to stick to my current plan and she also gave me coaching so that I could get into the right mindset.

She created some really amazing superset exercises, as she calls them, and taught me that I didn't really have to spend hours and hours exercising to get results. I found that the exercise programs that she created for me were fairly challenging but they were easy enough that even I could do it, so that was amazing and I feel like now I'm starting to get into a rhythm of exercise, so thank you so much, Robyn.

It's been amazing working with you and would I recommend Robyn? Absolutely, yes! Do not hesitate to reach out to her if you feel like you need to lose some weight, you need some motivation, don't know where to start with exercise or diet, she can really get you going in the right direction." Tina

Women come to me because they want to fit into their jeans, lose weight, get strong, feel fit and fabulous. They are ready to make the lifestyle changes needed for them to achieve their goals. I help them do this by showing them how to take small steps daily, then make those steps into habits that are easy and sustainable.

I encourage women to honour their body and treat it well with good quality nourishment, movement, stress reduction and sleep. It is my hope they recognise that they are the most important person in their lives and can achieve any goal they truly desire.

I help women to take control of their own health, strength and fitness and to be able to reach and maintain their desired body weight. I inspire them to take ACTION and CHOOSE to do something every single day which changes their lives for the better and helps them become the woman they've always wanted to be.

About the Author

Robyn is a Weight Loss and Strength Coach for women in midlife who has transformed her own life after years of obesity and processed food addiction. She now inspires and supports hundreds of women through her online programs and supportive communities.

She is the Founder of *Strong, Fit and Fabulous Women* and is passionate about helping women choose themselves, take action, and create sustainable change in their health, strength and confidence. Her mission is to positively impact over one million women to feel strong, capable and energised in their bodies.

Robyn is a certified Personal Trainer, Fitness Instructor and NLP Practitioner. She believes true vitality comes from strength training, nourishing nutrition, quality sleep and reducing stress, creating not just weight loss, but a renewed zest for life.

Outside of coaching, Robyn loves music and dance, and enjoys playing guitar and piano.

Facebook: www.facebook.com/Robynet

Facebook Group: Strong, Fit and Fabulous Women

Email: help@robyned.com

Stacey Ferguson

There were times I questioned whether my story was even worth sharing, unsure it was enough in a world that so often measures strength by the scale of suffering.

My story isn't one marked by one explosive moment or a single, defining trauma. There is no clear before and after, no moment where everything fell apart all at once. Instead, my story has been shaped by perseverance, by living through seasons where I held it all together and others where I couldn't. Seasons when life felt like it was unravelling around me, faster than I could keep up.

It's a story of growth and understanding built slowly over many years. A story of resilience formed by showing up most days, falling down some days and finding my feet again always. Not because I am strong, but because I chose to continue when strength felt so far away.

"Not all strength is loud. Sometimes it is the quiet voice that says, 'I will try again tomorrow.'"

~ Mary Anne Radmacher

Ever since I was a little girl I knew I wanted to be a Mum, not in the traditional sense, but a Mum who worked. Growing up in the late 80's, early 90s that wasn't something I seen very often, my own Mum stayed home, and there was nothing wrong with that – it was simply the world we lived in, it just made sense back then. But even from that young age I felt pulled towards a life that I could build that held both my family and my ambition. I didn't want motherhood to define me or replace who I was, but to expand who I could become.

When I was fourteen, my whole life changed. Our family of 7 moved from a busy town on the Central Coast of Queensland with a population of around 40,000 – to a tiny little outback town almost smack bang in the middle of Queensland with no more than 300 people. We'd visited a few times growing up, but I still didn't know what to expect but because Dad grew up there he knew what we were getting into. He promised us freedom, community and a kind of independence we had never known. I was excited for the move, but also terrified and heartbroken to be leaving all my friends and the only life I'd ever known.

This new town was exactly what they said it would be! From the moment we arrived it was obvious that everyone knew everyone. New friends were easy to make. Family was close by and before long, it felt like we had lived there my entire life. That little town shaped me in ways I didn't realise at the time. It taught me how to belong, how to adapt and how to find my place even when everything around me changed.

It was there I met my high school sweetheart, my now husband. We grew up fast. I moved in with his family when I was just 16. By the age of 17 we were renting our own home. We built a life together, bought a home and after 5 years we started to try for a baby. After years of trying, I fell pregnant with our son. A few months later we got engaged.

In 2011, our beautiful baby boy was born, via emergency caesarean. I had planned to take 12 months maternity leave, excited to soak in every little moment of that first year. But 10 months in, I got a call, I wasn't expecting. The manager of my workplace had suddenly left and they needed someone to step in. Someone reliable, someone who already knew the job. Someone who wouldn't say no. And even though it was earlier than we had planned and even though there was a part of me that wasn't quite ready, the people pleaser in me and the ambitious part of me both answered yes before I had a minute to think it through.

Within a few days, I was back in the office, stepping proudly into a version of myself I had imagined for years — a mum who worked, who contributed, who balanced it all. But the reality looked nothing like the picture I'd carried in my mind. Living in a small town meant there was no daycare, and even finding a babysitter was a challenge. We leaned on family when we could, but they had their own busy lives, which meant that some days my ten-month-old simply had to come to work with me.

Most days he sat on the floor behind the counter, surrounded by his toys, happily babbling to the locals as they came and went. He'd snack, play, or nap in his pram or the porta-cot I set up in the gallery — on the days I could get him to sleep at all. More often than not, I was holding him on my hip or rocking him in the pram while serving customers, typing one-handed or answering phones. People talk about mums being able to multitask, but this felt like the ultimate test — a crash course in doing everything at once, long before I realised the toll it would eventually take.

After a while, things started to settle into a little rhythm – a busy, messy, stretched-thin rhythm, but a rhythm all the same. We were young, building our lives in a small town, juggling work, a small business and a family. After a 3-year engagement, we were married in Townsville, the place that planted a quiet seed in me, a feeling that one day, somehow, this place would be home.

A few short months after our wedding - Ben's family was shaken by the sudden loss of his Uncle. Without hesitation Ben stepped in to help where he could driving for the family's transport company. Eventually this led to putting our business on hold so he could drive full-time for the family business. That's the kind of man Ben is, loyal and always the first to show up when he's needed.

What I didn't realise then was how much that decision shaped him and us. How deeply he felt the responsibility to show up. How he poured himself into keeping things going and how, later, when he eventually decided to step away and put our family and his needs first, the hurt that would leave a mark on him ran far deeper than anyone would ever see.

Somewhere in the middle of all that noise, we decided we were ready to grow our family. It didn't happen easily though – month after month passed, each one carrying its own quiet disappointment. And then, just as I was ready to give up and accept that we would only have one child, in late 2014, I finally fell pregnant. This pregnancy felt different, I was sicker, more exhausted and constantly queasy. As the pregnancy went on I had a little inkling of how full of life this little girl was going to be! As soon as I could feel her inside my stomach I swear she was doing cartwheels and flips, always wriggling. My sister-in-law often joking that it was a sign she was going to be a wild child – I don't think she's ever been more right in her life! Our beautiful baby girl hasn't slowed down since the day she was born! Always making us laugh, keeping us on our toes and knowing exactly who she is and what she wants.

On the outside everything looked exactly as it should. A growing family, a hardworking husband, a job I was committed to. A life that, from a distance, seemed to be unfolding exactly the way I'd always imagined. But underneath, something quieter was happening – a slow build up of pressure, exhaustion and expectation that I didn't yet recognise. I was still trying to be everything to everyone; the capable and present working Mum – returning to work just 4 months after the birth of our daughter, the supportive wife, the girl that never said no. I didn't realise then how much I was carrying, or how close I was to the moment that would change me for good.

Only a few months after our daughter was born we travelled away for a friend's birthday. I was so excited to be with friends and family, to have a little break from our regular routine. Marley and I drove the 6 hours on our own, meeting friends along the way to travel together. Ben and Levi followed in the truck, because if you know a truck driver, you know they will plan their social life around their truckin' life. Mum and her partner flew in from Brisbane to watch the kids for a night. Everything worked perfectly. It should've been a fun time away and for the most part it was.

On the Monday it was time to head home. Ben left early to load the truck and the kids and I headed to the shops to do what every country Mum does on a trip to the big smoke – stock up on everything we couldn't get at home. I pulled into the shopping centre, unloaded the pram, settled Marley in, grabbed Levi's hand and headed inside. Just an ordinary moment – one that had been done many times before.

But somewhere between the escalator and the aisles, something inside me faltered. I felt an uneasiness I had never felt before. I realised I needed a trolley to do the groceries, so I went to find one, while I was searching, I realised that I should probably take the pram back to the car. Then I wasn't sure. I walked in circles, pushing the pram with one hand, holding Levi's with the other. We eventually walked back to the car, loaded the pram in, then came back inside. I started looking for a trolley with a babyseat, it was like they didn't exist. In that moment, juggling a baby in my arms and my son's hand in mine, minutes felt like hours. My mind felt foggy, racing, disconnected, my stomach churned, my thoughts were scattered, almost like I was watching myself from the outside, unable to make the simplest decision.

It was such a small moment, so ordinary, so easy to dismiss. But standing there in that busy shopping centre surrounded by noise, people and bright lights I felt something I couldn't explain. A heaviness, a shakiness, a confusion. A sense that something wasn't quite right – something didn't feel the same. I didn't have words for it then, but that was the moment that everything changed. The moment I realised that something was wrong. The first crack in a foundation I'd spent years holding together.

I started to drive the 6 hours home but the tears wouldn't stop. Every kilometre felt like a struggle and eventually after 250km on the lonely road I had to call Ben, not knowing what to do or how to keep driving. He was in front of me by a few hours, so he waited for us in a small town, hoping that the one accommodation option in town had some availability. As we settled in for the night, I was still so unsure of what was happening, why couldn't I stop crying? What was wrong with me? Ben was confused too, when he had left me I was fine, happy, relaxed even. I can't even begin to imagine what was going through Levi's mind, watching his Mum sob uncontrollably, he was only four.

In the weeks, months and even years that followed, I continued to mask what I was feeling and just got on with life. I was a busy mum after all. I didn't think to seek professional help, I simply pushed the sadness aside or let it out by finding any excuse to yell and fight with Ben and if he wasn't home the kids copped it. I filled my days with work, social activities and volunteering where I could. I needed to keep busy, not realising then that it was a way of coping, avoiding being alone with my thoughts. Trying to get away from the monster I felt I was becoming. I surrounded myself with people, keeping my mind occupied. But at home in the darkness of the night or early mornings I struggled.

For a long time, I told myself this was just how life felt now, that everyone was tired, overwhelmed and carrying more than they let on. All Mum's lost their shit every day, right? I convinced myself I was fine because for the most part I was functioning. I was showing up. I was getting through the days. From the outside, life looked full and busy, even happy most of the time. But underneath it all, I was constantly running, from silence, from stillness, from frustration and from my own thoughts.

Partying became my escape. Noise became my comfort. If there were people around, music playing, plans to attend or things to organise, it meant I didn't have to sit with what I was feeling. I didn't have to risk starting another fight with Ben or yelling at the kids again. I filled every gap in my life with anything I could, saying yes to everything. It wasn't because I was thriving. It was because slowing down felt too heavy.

This pattern continued on for years. Eventually I reached a point where pushing through was no longer enough, I finally reached out for support – something I had never truly allowed myself to do before. It was there I began to understand the depth of what I was experiencing, I was diagnosed with major depression and for the first time so many pieces of my life began to make sense. I could trace the thread all the way back to those early years, to the shopping centre moment, to the confusion, the sadness, all the way back to postnatal depression. At first it felt like a failed moment, I hadn't been able to see it at the time but this was the turning point, the moment I began to trust the process of healing and growth. It was clarity and with that clarity became compassion for the woman I had been, doing her best to survive without the tools she needed. Looking back now, I can see I wasn't weak – I was coping the only way I knew how. I hadn't been taught how to process emotions or ask for help. I had learned to push through, hold it together and keep moving forward no matter what, so that's what I did.

In 2021, after feeling like I was getting my life back on track, I returned from a conference where I had felt more alive, more understood and more connected than I had in a long time, a moment happened that quietly changed me. A friend told me that I should keep my happiness to a minimum because I never know who could be struggling around me, that my happiness was too much, too visible, too loud. I don't believe those were the exact words or that they were meant to hurt me, but they landed deeply and without realising it, I began to shrink myself.

I dimmed my excitement, I softened my voice. I made myself smaller in spaces where I had once felt free to shine. Slowly, I lost pieces of who I was – not all at once, but little by little. The woman who had felt so full of possibility at that conference faded into someone who focused on staying comfortable for others instead of being honest with herself. I felt so alone.

In 2022 after spending most of my days in tears at work, I decided to step away for a year. I told myself it was time to focus on my small business, and to spend more time with the kids as our son stepped into high school. While that was partly true it was also a pause I didn't yet understand I needed. Even then my instinct was to still give – it filled me with joy to show up for others, but I wasn't showing up for myself first – so what I thought was filling my cup, hosting international women's day events, bringing women together, creating space for connection and conversation was actually draining me, although I couldn't see it then.

Then in 2023, we packed up our lives and moved to Townsville. The place that planted that seed almost exactly 10 years before had now sprouted. It was a fresh start, a chance to reset. While the move came with challenges of its own, it also created space – space to breathe, to reflect and to finally begin listening to myself.

Healing hasn't happened overnight, as a matter of fact, I am still healing today – but as the days go on it comes through learning, unlearning, self-awareness and choosing myself in ways I never had before. Slowly I have been rebuilding myself not just my strength, my confidence, my voice and my sense of worth. I stopped running from the quiet and started listening to it. I learned that growth isn't about becoming someone new, but about coming home to who I was always meant to be.

Today, I am not the woman I was in that shopping centre – but I honour her. Every hard season shapes me into someone more grounded, more intentional and more deeply connected to myself and others. I've learned that resilience isn't about never breaking; I still have hard moments, but it's about allowing myself to heal and rise again and again.

My journey isn't finished; it never will be. I am still growing, still healing and still becoming. Growth is something I now welcome, not fear. I continue to evolve, to reflect, to learn and to stretch beyond old limits. What once felt like my greatest struggle has become my greatest purpose.

That purpose now lives in empowering other women, creating spaces where stories are honoured, voices are heard and experiences are celebrated, whether they were shaped by quiet moments or life-altering ones. I want women to know their stories matter. That all women are worthy of being seen, their stories heard and their lives celebrated. Strength lives in every journey – the loud ones and the quiet ones alike.

Sometimes, the most powerful transformations don't begin with everything falling apart. Sometimes, they begin with a moment of awareness and the courage to keep going, to get back on your feet, time after time, no matter how far away strength feels.

About the Author

Stacey Ferguson is a wife, Mumma, storyteller and emerging author passionate about highlighting the quiet strength found in everyday lives. With a deep appreciation for growth, resilience and personal evolution, she holds a vision for creating spaces where women feel seen, heard and empowered to honour their own stories, even the ones that once felt ordinary or overlooked.

Having grown up in both a city and a small country town, Stacey's journey has shaped her perspective on change, courage and connection. She loves sharing her reflections and moments of life on social media, fostering honest and relatable conversations with women from all walks of life.

When she's not writing or creating, you'll often find Stacey enjoying time with her friends and family, playing cards, singing and her favourite thing of all, laughing and having fun.

Email: staceyfergusonjp@gmail.com

Facebook: www.facebook.com/stacey.james.77964

Instagram: www.instagram.com/staceyaferguson

Beverly Henaway

What is my purpose?

Twelve years earlier...

After the normal morning rush of getting my children and husband ready for school and work, I finally had time to myself; my favourite part of the day. In the quiet, I paused, and found myself asking, "What is my purpose?" My days felt the same, like I was stuck living on repeat. My world revolved around the happiness of my husband and children.

Sitting in that moment, a strange awkwardness filled the air because instead of answers, I found a long silence. Normally my mind was so hectic. But not this time. My mind was silent. Blank. Desperately looking inward for an answer, I discovered an emptiness and loneliness. I felt tired: not the type of tiredness that comes from lack of sleep but emotionally checked out like an empty shell, emotionless and numb.

Where was I, the young, happy, cheeky girl who always had a

huge imagination, the young girl who grew up surrounded by family, surrounded by love, laughter, and support?

Being the baby of the family came with special privileges. I knew I was the favourite child, able to charm my parents, older sister, and brother into giving me what I wanted, especially my eldest sister who often played the role of a second mother. When my mother passed away seven years earlier, her loss rocked our world. Our once tight-knit family, fell apart.

Since then, I have been trying to survive in a world without her, and without her guidance. Her correction was always done in love. Her presence always made me feel safe. My mother Marilyn Rebel was a strong Christian woman of faith who dedicated her life to God until her very last breath. I missed her hugs. I missed seeing her face light up as she shared about all the amazing ways God had blessed her and set her free from the addiction of alcohol and cigarettes, how He taught her to read and gave her the boldness to preach. I loved how she carried herself with grace and unshakable strength in the hard seasons of her life. When life knocked her down, she did not stay down for long. Even in the most heartbreaking and unimaginable season of her life, grieving the sudden loss of her son, my brother Mervyn, she stayed strong in her faith. She was a woman of influence and wisdom. Her life seemed far from boring.

Missing her like crazy is what compelled me to ask God, "What is my purpose?" I wanted more than the boring, mundane life I was stuck in. I thought if God could do all those amazing things in my mother's life, surely He could do something incredible in mine too.

Don't get me wrong! I love being a mother and a wife! My world revolved around them; their happiness was my daily goal. But sadly, somewhere between motherhood and marriage, trying to portray the perfect life to the outside world, I started to disappear. That day, twelve years ago, I had no idea what I was about to unlock when I asked, "What is my purpose?"

I once heard a preacher say, "Be careful what you ask for, you just might receive it, but not in the way you expect." Those words came to life, not straight away, but shortly after. My familiar, boring, safe world flipped 360: it became unpredictable. In a desperate plea for help, I separated from my husband. I didn't have the strength anymore to uphold the fakeness of perfection. The life I was living was hypocritical to the 'Christian' life I portrayed on social media and beyond the secrets of my walls. I attended my husband's family church, where his grandfather was the Pastor. I made sure my children and I looked the part but inside I silently struggled with alcohol addiction. I felt like a fraud every time I made a mix of my favourite drinks to unwind or drink away the frustrations of the week. My husband was also a heavy drinker and weed smoker. I didn't realise our marriage had been formed through trauma bonding and substance abuse. Alcohol became my escape, the only coping mechanism I knew and relied on.

My turning point came after a big night of drinking; I was extremely hungover. My head ached and I could barely move. I called out to my eldest son, who was eight, and gave him instructions to make his younger siblings breakfast. Seeing the sadness in his eyes and disappointment on his little face, made my heart fill with a hollow ache. I told myself this needs to stop! I need to stop drinking because my children's happiness is at stake.

I worked up the courage to talk to my husband about my decision to quit drinking. He did not take it well. After all, it was our trauma bonding ritual, our coping mechanism, our numbing tool, our normal. My husband wasn't ready for such a big change and why would he? He loved the life he had, and protecting it made sense to him. With no fight left in me, I decided it would be easier to leave. I longed for my mother's love and family support. Secretly the little girl in me was missing home.

Finding my purpose through the darkness

After I called my sister, crying, asking if we could move in, she sprang into action, squeezing a single bunk bed right beside her queen-sized bed. I moved in with my eldest sister, the one who had once devoted herself to me like a second mother. My sleeping / quiet area was the bunk bed; my two sons slept on the top bunk, and my two daughters and I shared the bottom bed. My only shield of peace was a sheet that I tucked under the top mattress as a wall or barrier of privacy.

Tucking my children in, the first night at my sister's, my youngest son asked me, "Mum, when are we going back home?" I tried my best to calmly reassure him, saying, "Soon son, this is only for a little while." I knew my other children were listening.

A wave of regret washed over me. Everything in me wanted to scream. I was minutes away from crumbling. As much as I wanted to give up, I couldn't. I can't remember if I slept that night - my mind flooded with 'what ifs'. Overwhelming regret and remorse echoed through my mind until morning. I walked away from a spacious four-bedroom home to seek support in a small, overcrowded three-bedroom house where nineteen of us - eight adults and eleven children - were crammed together like sardines with only one bathroom to share. The quietness I looked forward to after the morning school rush, no longer existed. My 'normal' no longer existed.

I began hearing wild stories of my husband partying in our home. It wasn't the thought of him enjoying himself in a spacious four-bedroom home that hurt – it was realising I was choosing to change, and I was doing this alone.

A couple of months later, my sister and I had a heart-to-heart conversation. I learned she, too, had not been the same since Mum's passing. She felt guilty for not being able to give me the support I needed; I didn't question her because I completely understood. That afternoon I caved. For the sake of my sanity and deep desire for peace and quiet, I humbled myself and moved back in with my husband. It did not take long to fall back to the façade of upholding the 'fake' picture-perfect family.

Over the following six years, it felt as if I was living in a heart-wrenching battlefield, constantly on alert. I walked on eggshells, terrified of saying something that could trigger my husband to have an outburst. Desperately hoping for things to get better, but sadly, deep down, I knew they wouldn't. The more I pushed for an alcohol-free home, the more my husband retaliated by partying. During the steady seasons, I found the strength to refuse alcohol, but through the stormy seasons, the fight and temptation overpowered me. I gave in.

I need to mention at this point, I continued attending church with my children. I volunteered to help lead and plan the kids' activities in Sunday School. Occasionally, my husband would join us.

On New Year's Eve, 2018, I was at my lowest. This rock bottom encounter was different to the ones I had previously experienced. It felt dangerous. My mind was dark. It was at this very moment I understood how good, strong women can end up in jail. I agreed to have a drink with my husband; he was so excited. But secretly, unbeknown to him, I was full of resentment and hate. I planned to act out and be a b..tch and ruin his night. My goal was to show him that if he chose a reckless party lifestyle, then this is the version of me he is choosing to live with.

My plan worked. We ended up in an explosive confrontation – it was the worst fight we had ever had. Everything I was holding in and wanted to say for years, came out. I am surprised the police were not called.

The next day, my eldest son, now twelve, walked into my room while I was sleeping and woke me up, crying. When I asked him why he was crying, he said that I had broken my promise: I promised him and my younger children that the drink before this one was my last. Seeing the disappointment in his eyes and the look of betrayal on his face, cut me deep. It took me back six years earlier when I had asked him to make breakfast for his younger siblings. My heart filled with the same hollow ache again. I told myself this really needs to stop! I need to stop drinking and break this cycle!

Feeling disheartened, I avoided my husband moving quietly through the house, tending to our children's needs. I needed time to think. I desperately wanted to leave again and get as far away from him as possible. But, I had nowhere to go. I felt stuck. The darkness that was in my mind had found its way to my heart. Depression consumed me. Feeling worn out, I started sobbing. Tears streamed down my face. In a desperate plea for help, I quietly prayed because I didn't know what else to do.

I can't remember every word. I remember saying something like, "Father God, please help me! Just like you took the desire of alcohol addiction away from my mother, please take it away from me too."

I also asked God to shine his light inside of me; to make a way for my situation to get better and for this to be the last time I end up in this dark place.

That Sunday, I rose early, carefully tiptoeing around, my heart racing with anticipation to get to church. My mind was made up; I was rededicating my life to God and this time I was not turning back. The addiction of alcohol had to go.

As I was getting my children ready, my husband walked into the room and asked, "Where are you going?" This was the first time he had spoken to me in days. Trying not to show him that his presence intimidated me, I said, "Church" and continued to get ready.

Buckling my youngest into her car seat, I caught my husband's cologne. Without a word, he slipped past me and sat in the front seat, dressed in his church clothes. The drive to church put me on edge. The silence was so loud I could hear my heart beating. We walked into his grandfather's church looking like the perfect family and sat together in the last row.

The moment finally came - the time when the pastor would invite people to come up for prayer. Not wanting to look like the only one with problems, I waited until I felt ready. I took a deep breath, nervously stood up, and walked to the front. Embarrassed, I stood there with my eyes closed and waited patiently as the pastor made his way through the prayer line to me. I felt someone grab my hand as I opened my eyes. My heart melted. I saw my daughter's tiny hand in mine and all my other children standing on both sides of me. Doing a silent head count to see if they were all there with me, my heart suddenly skipped a beat. Shocked! There he was, my husband, standing at the end of the line, holding my son's hand. My heart filled with all kinds of emotions.

That afternoon after church, my husband approached me with two cups of coffee and asked if we could talk. It became the most raw, honest conversation we had ever had. Through tears, I stood my ground and spoke my truth: I will no longer live in a home where alcohol had a place. I knew that if I wanted change, I had to initiate it. It was now or never. I offered him a pardon, acknowledging how big my request was, and told him that if he wasn't ready for change, I was willing to release him. He was free to live his life as he chose. My heart ached as I said it, knowing that love sometimes requires letting go.

When he chose us, I felt an overwhelming sense of relief. For the first time there was no fight; he acknowledged it was time to change. Neither of us realised the impact our agreement would have: doors of blessings opened, and the direction of our future shifted. One of them being our move to Emu Park, so close to the beach that we can hear the waves roar at night.

After three years in an alcohol-free home, our life finally felt stable and peaceful. I began to feel safe enough to let my guard down and stop living in survival mode.

Completely out of nowhere, with no warning, my niece and one of my daughters walked in while I was at work enjoying a hot coffee after breakfast club. Without hesitation, my niece bluntly asked me whether it was true that I hated Uncle Mervyn and always looked to fight him? Caught off guard and feeling blindsided, I reminded myself that I was at work or perhaps it was God? I did my best to compose myself as my inner rage ignited, so intense my face felt like it was on fire. I steadily instructed them to leave my office immediately. She had no understanding of the line she had just crossed. After they left, my inner rage gave way to grief. I completely unravelled and wept uncontrollably.

Mervyn is my brother. He had passed away in a car accident 20 years earlier. Reflecting on what just happened, I questioned myself, "Who would tell her that?". I knew it would have had to be a close family member. Still upset, it hit me that my niece and daughter represent my next generation and if I don't share my story about Mervyn and our relationship, that will be the version my grandchildren and great-grandchildren will grow up hearing.

I prayed again, "Father God, please help me tell my story. I don't want that to be the story my grandchildren hear of me and Merv's relationship."

It was this simple prayer that awakened my purpose, the very question I'd asked myself twelve years ago.

Walking in my purpose

I didn't realise that being blindsided by my niece would push me towards seeking justice which ended up becoming the most important turning point in my life, one I now cherish deeply. I never imagined God would help me share my story through an early intervention well-being program.

I thought my story was meant just for family and my future generations, but now I can see it has the potential to touch countless lives around the world.

I am in awe of what God is doing, the transformation I have witnessed in my life, my husband and our children's lives, stands as a testament to all who know us.

My purpose that has awoken in me is called SCARS.

SCARS is a seven-step healing program where I share the path I walked after losing my brother and late mother.

SCARS began as a seed, planted deep in darkness, quietly growing in strength and resilience, watered by tears, time, trouble and endurance, tested by changing seasons. The path I walked was not easy. Around each corner lay rough, unfamiliar ground, only the bravest dared to walk, it left its marks, bruises and scars.

Now that I have made it through, part of my purpose is to turn back, walking in my purpose by retracing my steps into those dark places that once broke me, searching for women who are stuck, trapped in the lie that there is no way out. Their silent cries for help stirs something deep within me because I was once one of them.

It's also about transforming heartbreak into self-discovery and helping others to reclaim their identity after loss through a wound-to-scar template I created. I learned that losing a loved one can trigger an identity crisis - I experienced this after my mother passed, having always defined myself as her daughter.

In writing this, I realized the character I once admired in my mother is beginning to reveal itself in me: the strong woman of faith, who carries herself with grace and unshakeable strength through the hard seasons of her life; the woman who, when life knocks her down, rises - every time; the woman who always turns to God for help, and who, in return, took away her addiction to alcohol and turned her scars into something beautiful; the woman of influence and wisdom, whose life is far from boring.

I chose to name my program SCARS because we all carry them and each scar holds a story of healing, resilience and hope.

My SCARS template:

1. Wound

2. Blood

3. Add pressure

4. Scab

5. Itch

6. Healing

7. Scar

Since delivering my first workshop in 2022, SCARS has been embraced by many. I am often told my message is powerful because it resonates deeply with those who have experienced loss.

Get ready! Later this year, **Yarnz with Bev** is hitting the road, for adventure, family fun and workshops wherever we go.

About the Author

Beverley Henaway is the founder and owner of *Yarnz with Bev*. She is a proud mother of six, grandmother and a devoted wife; a strong-spirited Aboriginal woman from the Iman and Bidjara tribes around Central Queensland. Beverley's work is grounded in compassion, storytelling, and deep understanding, supporting women from all walks of life on their journeys toward self-discovery, resilience, and wellbeing.

Drawing from her lived experience of loss, grief, and recovery from substance abuse, Beverley has transformed pain into purpose. She is a life coach who has empowered and inspired women to look within, reconnect with themselves, and reclaim their power through her intervention wellbeing programs, SCARS and ROOM, the first of many she plans to develop. Beverley loves supporting her daughters' netball journey and is deeply connected to her family. She is excited to grow Yarnz with Bev into a family enterprise, a legacy for her next generation.

Facebook: www.facebook.com/p/Yarnz-With-Bev-100087605784490

Email: yarnzwithbev@outlook.com

Rachel Marion Judd

Beyond Healing: Coming Back
to Myself

A story of how an identity is formed, how I learned to love myself again, and how I chose to live with clarity, coherence, and alignment with my unique design

For a long time, I believed that something in me needed fixing. What I didn't yet understand was that what I really needed was to come back to myself.

On the surface, my life appeared functional and intact. I was capable, responsible, and getting on with things. I had learned how to cope well, how to keep moving, how to adapt. Capability became part of how I was known. I was reliable, steady, and expected to manage. That way of being was rewarded, affirmed, and quietly reinforced.

Strength, as I understood it then, meant not needing much, not asking questions, and not slowing down. I didn't know how to recognise my own needs, or how to name them. I responded to what was required, and to the people who were counting on me.

Over time, responding to everyone else became a substitute for connection with myself. I mistook endurance for identity, and functionality for wholeness. There was no language then for what was missing, only a sense that something essential had been set aside in order to keep going. What surfaced next wasn't something new. It was something that had been waiting quietly for years.

I share this not because my story is finished, nor is it mine to keep, but in the hope it may be useful to someone who needs it.

Seventeen years earlier, something had happened that I believed I had already dealt with. By the time it resurfaced, I was thirty-four, newly married and settling into our new home. I was living a full life, functioning well, and believing the past was behind me. For a long time, my sense of self had been shaped by coping rather than choice.

What I couldn't yet understand at that age was how much I was carrying quietly, without the space or support to feel it, and how far I had moved away from myself in order to survive. It was this quiet disconnection that eventually led me to counselling. Not because my life had fallen apart, but because something within me was asking to be acknowledged. In that space, I began to see that surviving had required me to stay functional and composed, often at the expense of my own inner world.

Counselling didn't pull me back into the past. It gave me a place to meet myself differently. Slowly, I began to find a voice that wasn't just factual or detached, but connected. One that could hold truth without collapsing under it.

There was also further sexual abuse in my late twenties while I was living and teaching in London. It compounded what I had already learned to carry, quietly eroding my sense of pride, self-worth, and trust in myself. A year later, I met the man who would become my husband and the father of my children. At the time, I did not recognise how much my choices were still being shaped by survival rather than self. Even after the marriage ended, that pattern persisted. I continued to attract relationships that mirrored manipulation and emotional harm, reinforcing beliefs about my worth that had been formed long before. What I was living was not a coincidence. It was conditioning. What stayed with me most was not only what had happened, but the meaning I quietly attached to it about myself.

Each experience shaped how I came to understand my worth, my safety, and what I could expect in relationships. I wasn't alert or grounded; I was numb and largely disconnected from myself. Without self-confidence or boundaries to protect myself, I was drawn into relationships that repeated familiar harm. What felt familiar wasn't what was healthy, but what I had learned to endure.

When the marriage ended in February 2015, my world reorganised itself around survival in a very practical way. By December that year, I had relocated with my two young children to Bendigo, three hours away from the life we had known. My focus became singular and unwavering: keeping them safe, creating stability, and making sure life continued.

In that season, there was little space left for me. I became a mother, a provider, a carer, and a steady presence — whatever was required. Responsibility shaped my days, and coping shaped my identity.

The years that followed were not marked by crisis, but by continuity. Life moved forward in practical ways. The children grew. Responsibilities shifted. I functioned. From the outside, there was nothing to fix. Inside, however, something essential was slipping away. I had lost myself, along with any clear sense of identity or direction. Survival had become a way of being, not a temporary state. When life requires you to keep moving, reflection becomes a luxury.

I learned how to carry on as though I was okay, often for the sake of others, while my own internal sense of direction quietly faded. Over time, I became more withdrawn and less curious, without a clear focus. I was exhausted and overwhelmed, and it was only by turning inward and seeking support that healing and understanding began.

It was then that I began to see the patterns that had shaped me over time. I recognised how often I had made decisions based on what was required of me rather than what felt aligned. I adapted quickly, adjusted expectations, and minimised my own needs without questioning why.

I came to understand that identity is not formed only through single events, but through repetition. Through what we learn to tolerate. Through what we gradually abandon in ourselves. The version of myself I had been living from was not chosen consciously. It had been shaped quietly, reinforced by years of responsibility, quiet self-abandonment, and self-sacrifice.

Seeing this didn't undo the past, but it gave me language and awareness. I could name patterns, distinguish past from present, and articulate my experience without collapsing into it. And with that came choice — and with choice, the possibility of change.

In the years that followed, I began slowly and deliberately to prioritise working on myself. This wasn't a dramatic turning point, but a series of conscious steps taken alongside the demands of daily life. I participated in group programs focused on domestic violence and recovery after separation, spaces where my experiences were no longer isolated or unnamed. Later, through transformational work with Landmark, I encountered a distinction that stayed with me: separating what had happened from the stories I had carried about what it meant. That work didn't erase the past, but it loosened its grip. For the first time, I could see how meaning had shaped my identity — and that meaning could be questioned.

Around two years ago, I entered a deeper phase of work that asked more of me than insight alone. Through coaching, NLP, and emotional release processes, I revisited my past not to relive it, but to reorganise how it lived within me.

What emerged wasn't blame or collapse, but clarity. I recognised patterns that were no longer necessary, beliefs that were never truly mine, and ways of being that had formed around survival rather than truth. By this point, I wasn't undoing my past. I was creating the internal conditions to live differently.

While coaching and NLP supported my healing and deepened my self-awareness, it was my study of Human Design that truly changed my trajectory. I felt broken and directionless until I realised I had been living a life that wasn't working for me.

For the first time, I could see how I had been living in misalignment — and why life had so often felt forced, mismatched, or out of sync. It wasn't that I was broken or doing life incorrectly. I was simply trying to live in ways that were not aligned with how I am designed to operate. Understanding this brought an unexpected sense of ease and calm. I no longer felt the need to force myself into ways of working that were never designed for me. Instead, I had a clear internal reference point.

Human Design has since become a beacon for how I live, decide, rest, and move forward — not as a rigid system, but as a framework that honours coherence over effort. As this understanding settled in my own life, I began to notice similar shifts emerging in the women I worked alongside. Often, they came to our conversations with a quiet sense that something needed to change, even if they couldn't yet name what that change was.

There was rarely a dramatic turning point. More often, it was a feeling of being out of sync with themselves, unsure how to move forward once survival was no longer the organising force of their lives.

What tended to unfold was not a sudden breakthrough, but a steadier relationship with themselves. As we slowed things down, patterns became easier to recognise. Decisions that had once felt overwhelming could be approached with more calm and perspective. Rather than trying to fix anything, the work invited reflection, awareness, and choice.

Reflecting on her experience, Rachael shared, *"Rather than being directed or 'fixed,' I felt guided to arrive at my own insights, which made the changes feel sustainable and genuinely my own."*

Another woman shared, *"Rachel allowed me the space to come to realisations on my own and guided me through releasing the emotional weight I'd been carrying for most of my life."*

Again and again, I saw that meaningful shifts came from

understanding rather than effort. From recognising patterns, identifying misalignment, and giving ourselves permission to live differently. When women began to see that their exhaustion was not a personal failure, but a signal of sustained adaptation, something softened. Self-judgement gave way to curiosity. Coping gave way to choice. Alignment is not about becoming someone new or forcing change. It is about returning to what has always been there, and allowing life to be lived with greater coherence, steadiness, and self-trust.

What I am increasingly aware of is how many women reach a point where healing has done its work, yet life still feels strangely incomplete. The urgency has eased. The intensity has passed. From the outside, things appear stable again. And yet internally, a quiet question remains: *How do I live now?*

This is the space I recognise deeply — the space after survival, but before orientation. Where familiar coping strategies no longer fit, yet new ways of being have not fully formed.

For many women, this phase arrives alongside profound life transitions: motherhood and the reshaping of identity that follows; separation or divorce and the reorganisation of self that comes with it; returning to work after years of caring for others; navigating peri-menopause and menopause, with the cognitive, emotional, and physical shifts that can leave women feeling unfamiliar to themselves.

On the surface, these experiences look different. Underneath, they share a common thread: a loss of internal reference. Again and again, I have seen how easily women assume this disorientation means something is wrong with them. That they should be further along, more certain, more motivated.

In truth, what is often missing is not resilience or effort, but coherence — an understanding of how they are designed to operate, decide, rest, and move forward in a way that honours their own rhythms rather than overriding them.

Healing alone does not teach us how to live in alignment. It restores capacity, but it does not always provide direction. Many women reach a threshold where they are no longer in crisis, yet not yet oriented toward what comes next. This is not a problem to solve. It is an invitation.

This is where I now see my work extending. Supporting women to reconnect with themselves, understand their unique design, and integrate healing with practical direction. To move from coping into conscious choice. To design lives and businesses that honour their energy, timing, nervous systems, and seasons of life.

My vision is to work with women navigating identity shifts, midlife transitions, separation, burnout, and the quiet disorientation that can arise when old roles fall away. To support them not just to heal, but to live with clarity, coherence, and meaning, in ways that feel sustainable and true.

I am not here to tell women who to become. I am here to help them remember who they already are.

Coming back to myself changed everything.

— **Rachel Marion Judd**

About the Author

Rachel Marion Judd is a Reconnection Coach supporting women who have moved through significant life transitions and are seeking clarity, coherence, and a more meaningful way of living. Her work brings together lived experience, life coaching, NLP, Human Design, and breathwork to help women reconnect with themselves and realign with how they are naturally designed to operate.

Rachel works with women navigating identity shifts such as motherhood, separation or divorce, returning to work, burnout, and the transitions that often arise during peri-menopause and menopause. She supports women to move beyond coping, understand why life has felt misaligned or out of sync, and begin living with greater ease, self-trust, and internal direction.

A former primary and secondary teacher with a background in Visual Arts and Design, Rachel is also the mother of two teenagers and continues to draw inspiration from creativity, travel, and lived experience.

Facebook: www.facebook.com/rachel.marion.26

Email: info@rachelmarion.com

Website: rachelmarion.com

Jade McLachlan

What if no one is coming to save you… And the power has always been within?

Have you ever felt like you can't keep going on like this?

Some days it feels like you're drowning. Other days, the water sits just above your chest, and every step forward feels heavy. On the days it only reaches your waist or your knees, those feel like easier days.

If this feels familiar, you are not alone. I see you. I hear you. I understand.

I used to carry shame and guilt for admitting those feelings because I lacked understanding, compassion, and self-love for myself. At the time, I didn't know I was neurodivergent. On the outside, my life looked full—a supportive husband, two wonderful children, a home, a career, family, and friends. It was never perfect, but then again, whose life is?

As I sat in my living room with a cup of coffee warming my hands, exhaustion settled deep into my body - the kind that had been building for weeks, months, years, even. Tears rolled quietly down my face as I realised I had pushed myself to burnout. Again.

I've dedicated over twenty years to a profession I care deeply about—one I'm genuinely passionate about. But I've also been running for a long time. Each time overwhelm grew or relationships became challenging, I looked for the next opportunity, the next role, the next promotion.

Each time I heard the same words—*too sensitive, too defensive, always overthinking*—it left me feeling like I didn't belong, like no one truly understood me. When I tried to explain myself, I was told I was becoming aggressive. So I learned to be quiet. To soften my tone. To monitor my facial expressions and body language. To make myself smaller.

I became hyper-aware of everything—the slightest shift in tone, a look held a moment too long, a subtle change in posture. That constant vigilance was exhausting. It made me want to give up.

Over the years, proving my value became my driving force. I swallowed my needs, ignored my boundaries, and learned to doubt myself. My body held the tension—a knot in my stomach that never quite loosened, shoulders tight, breath shallow, always alert. Eventually, it could carry no more.

I've spent years trying to fit myself into neurotypical expectations, wearing a mask that no longer fits. Lately, it's been slipping, and I no longer have the energy to hold it in place—especially since receiving my ADHD diagnosis just over a year and a half ago, at the age of 38.

In the stillness, my internal dialogue grew louder. I can't keep living like this—the cycles of depression, anxiety, and the constant feeling of *I'm not good enough*, as I tried to hold everything together: being a mum, working full time as a leader and early years educator, showing up as a wife, friend, and daughter… and managing the hormones.

The striving. The adjusting. The endless cycle of pushing, crashing, recovering, and starting all over again. It felt relentless. Unmanageable.

Something had to change.

And as my thoughts continued to race, a memory surfaced—one I hadn't thought about in years.

After the birth of my first child, I was treated for postnatal depression. Looking back now, I can see that I had been struggling long before that. Over the years, I accessed counselling and medication, which supported me through difficult periods, even if their relief was mostly short-term.

I remembered one moment clearly. After my daughter was born, my doctor was worried about me. I wasn't coping. She looked perfect, and I felt like a nervous wreck - it felt like my sole job was to keep her alive.

He asked, *"Who is the most important person in your life?"* I said, *"My daughter."* He replied, *"No, you are. Because if you can't look after yourself, you won't be able to look after her."*

At the time, it didn't land. I had learned to put everyone else first.

Now, seventeen years later, as I sat with a cup of coffee, those words returned. As I finished my coffee, the realisation landed — clear and confronting: no one is coming to save me. No one really can. And that is where my power begins.

For the first time, I gave myself permission to rest—not as a reward, not because everything was done, but because my body could no longer continue the way it had been. I listened, really listened, without judgment, to what my body was asking of me. I chose myself. It felt strange, scary, and empowering all at once. Quietly, I praised myself for putting my needs first.

I stopped pushing through. I stopped overriding the signals. I allowed myself to pause.

What if the moment everything began to change wasn't loud or dramatic, but quiet—and deeply personal?

Choosing rest was not a weakness. It was honesty. It was self-respect. It was the moment I chose myself and put myself first.

It felt unfamiliar—I had never decided that before. It was new. And with that newness came a mix of empowerment, fear, and relief, all at once. Questions crept in: *What would people say? Would I be judged?*

But I was so exhausted—depressed, burnt out, and tearful—that I no longer had the energy to care. Rest wasn't a choice anymore; it was a necessity.

A couple of days later, as I scrolled through social media, I kept noticing the same advert. Normally, I would have scrolled straight past, but this time something felt different—something kept tugging at me. It was a four-day masterclass offering insight into the subconscious and a way to go deeper than just coping, to address what was really holding me back.

I thought, *why not?* I was naturally sceptical, but I was also open to trying something different. Somewhere deep inside, there was a part of me that wasn't willing to give up—a part a previous therapist once described as tenacity. This time, it showed up as a readiness to explore how my past experiences had quietly shaped the beliefs I lived by, the emotions I carried, and the decisions I made. Beliefs like *I'm not good enough, I have to put everyone else first, I must control everything to be safe,* and *my voice doesn't matter*—all of which had guided my life for far too long.

The masterclass was transformational for me. My sceptical, inquisitive mind needed tangible evidence.

On the fourth day, the founder guided us through a session where we were invited to choose something to eliminate from our lives that negatively impacted us. Nothing came to mind immediately—thinking on the spot had never been my strength.

As I scanned the chat online, I noticed people mentioning coffee. That's when it clicked—sugar. Cakes, chocolate, biscuits, syrup-laced coffees. After all, we all know that too much sugar in our diets isn't good for us.

The very next day, I noticed something unexpected—I didn't have any cravings. I hadn't reached for my evening biscuit with tea. I skipped my usual Irn-Bru with dinner. I even stopped drinking my morning and afternoon coffee—something I relied on daily. I didn't say it out loud, but inside I was thinking, *What's going on? This felt strange. This had never happened before.*

As the days went on and the cravings didn't return, confusion gave way to sadness for choosing something I enjoyed to eliminate. With Christmas and my birthday approaching, I wondered if this meant I'd lose the joy of afternoon tea with friends, festive treats, and birthday cake. Then, after speaking with someone in the training community, it clicked.

My brain needed proof. I needed to experience change—not just understand it intellectually—to trust that this work was worth my time, energy, and investment. In that moment, I began to glimpse the potential of this modality—not just to manage habits, but to create change at a deeper, subconscious level. Letting go of something I had depended on daily was the evidence I didn't know I needed.

Alongside that clarity came apprehension, anxiety, and fear. I was stepping into something unfamiliar, new, and that scared me. But it also felt honest. That tension—between fear and knowing—was what led me to sign up to train in this modality myself.

Through the training, I learn how the subconscious stores memories alongside the emotions we attach to them. Those emotions shape our beliefs, and over time, those beliefs quietly guide how we respond to the world—often without realising it. During my first facilitation as a trainee, my subconscious takes me back to an early postnatal moment I haven't consciously revisited in years. What surfaces isn't the event itself, but the emotions I have been carrying—anxiety, self-blame, and the belief that my needs don't matter.

In its place comes permission—to honour my boundaries, trust my voice, and recognise my resilience. I see that these shifts aren't just about letting go of discomfort; they are about consciously choosing what I strengthen in its place. I am actively creating the life I want: speaking up without fear, making choices aligned with my needs, and moving through the world with a calm confidence I am still growing into. Realising that I have agency over my internal world is quietly, profoundly transformative.

As the session comes to a close, something shifts. The emotional charge is released. My body feels lighter, more open. My energy changes, my face softens and brightens, and I feel a sense of ease I haven't felt in years. I can breathe more freely, my shoulders no longer feel heavy, and there is a subtle, undeniable lightness in my steps. Alongside that comes a renewed enthusiasm for life — subtle at first, but unmistakable.

That first release is only the beginning. In the sessions that follow, I work on long-held beliefs that have quietly shaped my life: "I'm not good enough," "I must put everyone else first," "I have to control everything to be safe," and "My voice doesn't matter." With each shift, I experience not only relief from old patterns, but a growing sense of clarity, agency, and empowerment — felt in my body as much as my mind.

With these changes settling in, a quieter understanding starts to emerge.

I believe everything happens for a reason, and that I was meant to come across this modality when I did. Before this work, I was moving through life from a place of victimhood and blame. Those emotions were held deeply in my body, and without realising it, they kept me stuck and unable to move forward. I haven't forgotten what has happened in my past, but I no longer see those experiences as something that defines or limits me. I now see them as lessons that have shaped my growth.

This modality has given me the tools and strategies to understand the negative beliefs my body has been holding onto for years. For a long time, my body felt heavy, and I didn't realise how much those beliefs were weighing me down or holding me back.

Through this work, I've learned how to release what no longer serves me and consciously choose the beliefs I want to store in my subconscious. That shift has allowed me to move from years of victimhood and blame into a place of reclaiming my power and taking control of my life.

For the first time, I can see myself clearly. I truly believe in myself. I love who I am — something I wasn't able to feel before. I know I'm still growing — life will always ask that of me — but I'm no longer standing still. There's forward movement now, and that shift feels deeply empowering.

I feel capable. I feel confident. I know that my worth, my value, and my voice matter. I feel strong within myself, and I trust my ability to set boundaries that protect both me and my energy as I continue to move forward.

I allow that inner strength to be felt, supported, and lived.

As I enter my Sunday reset class, I'm greeted warmly by the instructors and familiar faces. Twinkly lights cast a soft glow across the room, mats are laid out with cosy blankets and pillows, and affirmation cards sit gently on each mat. I choose one, and the message resonates, uplifting me before the work even begins.

The class begins with breathwork, accompanied by the subtle, relaxing sound of meditative music in the background. I feel the tension I was holding start to ease. Each inhale fills me with calm, and each exhale releases a little of the old stress and worry. As I breathe, I visualise a warm, steady light moving through my body, softening what feels tight and heavy.

Sound healing follows. The vibrations move through me in a way that words can't capture. I notice subtle shifts — my chest opens, my shoulders loosen, and a quiet energy hums through my body. It's grounding, energising, and deeply restorative. By the end, my body feels lighter and more open, my mind quieter, and I feel ready to step into the week with clarity and ease.

Beyond the Sunday reset, I've also joined a savasana sound bath and ritual class on Thursdays and a nature walk on Sunday mornings — all with the same supportive community. I try to attend these sessions as often as I can, offering myself consistency and intentional acts of self-love, and gentle ways to reconnect with my body, my mind, and the women I share this journey with.

After each session, we gather with herbal teas, sharing how we feel without judgment. We exchange tips, support, and encouragement. Listening to other women's breakthroughs, witnessing their courage, and sharing my own reflections reinforces my sense of agency and reminds me that growth is a shared journey.

These sessions — the breath, the sound, the movement, the walks, the gentle reflection, the laughter, the community — help me integrate the changes I'm making in my life. In being present, listening deeply, and holding space with understanding and compassion, I notice something shift in me, too. I see how much connection matters, how powerful it is to simply be heard, and I realise that I want to explore supporting others further — not by fixing, but by offering a listening ear, an open heart, and a space where people feel understood.

From that place of steadiness, I begin to notice how these shifts show up in my work with others.

What I'm learning is that people often arrive carrying discomfort or uncertainty, without fully understanding what's sitting underneath it. One of the first people I worked with came in carrying discomfort and anxiety, convinced the issue was about confidence and taking the next step in their business. By listening deeply and trusting my intuition, I was able to guide them beyond the surface concern and towards what was really holding them back.

What followed was almost immediate. Within minutes of finishing our session, they took action in a way they hadn't managed for a long time — reaching out to people, using their voice, and moving forward without the familiar fear of judgment. Watching that shift unfold reminded me how powerful it is when someone feels genuinely supported and understood, rather than pushed or fixed.

In another session, my client arrived feeling stuck and unsure, carrying anxiety and self-doubt beneath the surface. By creating a calm, steady environment where she felt safe to explore what lay underneath, she gained clarity and moved forward feeling lighter and more confident. The shift wasn't dramatic — it showed up in her calmness, awareness, and ability to take action.

I've also experienced the impact of connection beyond a single session. A woman reached out after seeing me speak openly about my own journey, particularly around neurodivergence. She shared how deeply she resonated with my experience and how, through our conversations, she finally felt seen and understood. That sense of recognition gave her the confidence to explore her own path more fully and take steps she had been uncertain about for years. Knowing that my openness could offer reassurance, clarity, and courage to someone else was incredibly meaningful.

These moments have shown me that real impact often happens quietly, when people feel safe enough to meet themselves honestly and realise they are more capable than they ever believed.

What connects all of these experiences is not the process alone, but the presence within it. Listening without judgement. Holding space with care. Trusting intuition. In each case, the movement forward happens when someone reconnects with their own inner clarity, confidence, and capacity to choose differently.

Alongside this, my own sense of direction continues to deepen. As I near facilitator accreditation in this modality, I feel a strong commitment to continuing my training so I can offer deeper guidance and support — both for myself and for others. I will be moving into advanced training, allowing me to hold more nuanced and complex work with integrity, care, and confidence.

Neurodivergence has been a significant part of my own journey, and it naturally shapes the way I support others. In the near future, I plan to train in an ADHD coaching programme to expand my knowledge and skill set further. This feels like a natural extension of the work I'm already doing — deepening my understanding so I can offer support that is informed, compassionate, and truly aligned with how neurodivergent minds and nervous systems work.

Looking ahead, my intention isn't to build something loud or performative, but something grounded and meaningful. I want to continue creating spaces where people don't need to over-explain, where they feel genuinely seen and understood, and where growth feels supported rather than overwhelming.

I believe the wider impact of this work happens quietly. When one person begins to trust themselves, they show up differently — in their relationships, their families, their work, and their communities. Those shifts ripple outward in ways that can't always be measured, but can be deeply felt. It's within those quiet ripples that I see the kind of impact I want to continue creating.

If my story began in a place of feeling overwhelmed and barely keeping my head above water, it now continues from a steadier place. One where I am grounded, present, and able to move forward — and where I can walk alongside others as they find their footing too.

If you see yourself in any part of this story — in the exhaustion, the doubt, or the quiet hope that something could be different — I want you to know this: I see you. I hear you. I understand you.

You don't need to explain yourself here.

You are enough. And I believe in you.

About the Author

Jade McLachlan is a late-diagnosed ADHD woman whose journey of self-discovery has led to deep self-acceptance, compassion, and reconnection with herself. Through this lived experience, she now supports other neurodivergent women to cultivate self-understanding, confidence, and a renewed sense of agency.

Jade is known for her calm, intuitive approach and her ability to create safe, inclusive spaces where individuals feel genuinely seen, heard, and empowered to move beyond long-held beliefs and take meaningful, self-led action. With over twenty years of professional experience, her work is grounded in leadership, coaching, and reflective practice within people-centred settings, alongside formal training and advanced study in Belief Coding®, with further professional development planned in ADHD coaching.

Outside of her professional life, Jade enjoys travelling—recently embracing European city day trips—alongside spa days, afternoon tea with friends, and spending quality time with her family through shared meals and game nights at home.

Instagram: www.instagram.com/unmaskedandrisingwithadhd

Facebook: www.facebook.com/jade.mclachlan.129

Email: jade@unmaskedandrising.com

Catherine Parkes

Have you ever been called crazy?

I Love Me Anyway was born at a time I believed was life's rock bottom. I was wrong.

My marriage and my family were in severe trouble, and it was not safe. My physical health had deteriorated to the point medical professionals were concerned I might not survive. My mental health had deteriorated to the point that I rarely left the bedroom. If I did, it was usually to go to the toilet or to cook dinner for my family. My children were repeatedly told, "Stay away from your mother. She's sick."

I was being controlled in every sense, financially, physically, emotionally, sexually. My access to money, decisions, rest, information, and safety was restricted. My reality was questioned constantly. My exhaustion was used as evidence against me. Like many people living under coercive control, I learned quickly that survival required silence, compliance, and performance.

In my isolation, I found a spiritual practice online, guided by a teacher on the other side of the world, both magical and scientific in her approach, and it offered me something I had not felt in a long time: a small amount of joy. More importantly, it offered education around boundaries, self-worth, and leadership. It helped me remember that I was a person.

That, too, became a problem. I was criticised for being "constantly in the room with her." A practice that grounded me was reframed as avoidance, obsession, and instability. Any step toward autonomy was treated as evidence of dysfunction.

When I attempted to flee domestic violence, I did not step into safety. I stepped into another system of control. My attempt to leave was misrepresented, and I found myself in legal trouble. At a critical moment, I was given very good legal advice to have my husband charged with domestic violence and to present to the courts that my mental health deterioration was the result of sustained fear and coercive control. I refused. I refused not because it was untrue, but because I understood something the system did not. I knew that charging him would not protect my children. It would endanger them. I knew that being labelled mentally unwell in court would not bring support. It would be used to discredit my parenting. I knew that once the narrative of instability was fixed to me, it would never be removed.

So instead, I protected the perpetrator. From day one, that was my role. The package deal included epilepsy. Seizures were frequent and unpredictable, woven into our family's daily life. It was my job to keep him alive. My nervous system learned to stay alert at all times. Caretaking was not an act of love. It was a survival requirement. I became codependent in a context that demanded it. My finances were controlled. My home was not in my name, even though I had paid for every part of it. I was socially isolated. And like many people in similar situations, I wore the labels pinned onto me: anxiety, depression, mental illness, physical illness, bad parent, bad partner, bad child. Never good enough. Never believed. Never safe.

There is a myth that leaving domestic violence is the hardest part. In my experience, leaving was only the beginning. Once I was no longer contained within one person's control, I became exposed to multiple systems. Legal. Policing. Child protection. Housing. Health. None of them connected, each asking different questions while ignoring the harm we were living with.

I was navigating these systems alone: underrepresented, financially depleted, unwell, and responsible for children who were also traumatised and exhibiting behaviours consistent with that trauma. Every form, interview, and interaction carried risk. A single misstep could and often did have long-term consequences. The system required me to be calm while reliving trauma, coherent while exhausted, compliant while unsafe.

Trauma was inconvenient. Fear was misread as instability. Protective behaviour became an obstruction. And parents who did not perform gratitude for minimal support were seen as difficult. The system assumes capacity from people it has already broken.

For a long time, I believed I was a personal target. That somehow I had failed in a uniquely spectacular way, or that I had been singled out for punishment, isolated to me or my little seaside hometown. It was only when I began quietly networking and speaking with others that I understood the truth. These failures were not isolated to me, or even to my country. Parents, women, men, and children in the United Kingdom and the United States were describing the same patterns, the same language, the same outcomes. Different laws, different accents, the same harm.

One of the most confronting realities I faced was discovering how many services designed to protect people are structured in ways that actively cause harm.

Women's refuges, for example, routinely refuse boys over the age of ten. Parents are forced to choose between their own safety and keeping their families together. Boys who have already witnessed violence are excluded at the very moment they need stability. Family separation is framed as policy necessity rather than recognised as trauma.

Police responses were similarly inconsistent. Some officers were kind but constrained. Others minimised, delayed, or redirected responsibility. Domestic violence was treated as a series of isolated incidents rather than a pattern of coercive control. Risk was assessed in moments, not in context.

Child Safety involvement was perhaps the most damaging. I experienced a system that facilitated ongoing contact with the perpetrator while scrutinising my every action. A system that interpreted my fear as instability, my protectiveness as hostility, and my exhaustion as incapacity. A system that rewarded compliance over truth.

The message was clear. If you want support, you must not make us uncomfortable. If you want safety, you must not name harm too loudly. This was not protection. It was administrative violence, harm delivered through process, policy, and indifference.

What is rarely discussed is the long-term damage created by these systems. The impact on my children has not passed. It shows up in their nervous systems, their sleep, their learning, their trust. It shows up in hypervigilance and withdrawal, in anger and grief. These are not individual failings. They are predictable outcomes of prolonged exposure to threat and instability.

For me, the damage was cumulative. Chronic health issues worsened. Trust in authority eroded. Financial recovery became more difficult the longer instability persisted. Opportunities were lost not because of a lack of ability, but because survival consumed all available energy. This is not resilience building.

This is harm compounding. Generational trauma is not only created by violence in the home. It is reinforced by systems that respond to that violence with fragmentation, disbelief, and punishment.

We talk a great deal now about safety, and rightly so. Around the world, there has been important progress in recognising domestic violence, naming harm, and acknowledging the long-term impact of trauma. This work matters. It has shifted awareness and saved lives. But balance matters too, and balance is where we are still falling short.

Global research shows that emotional and physical safety is not reaching all children equally. Boys, in particular, are more likely to express distress through external behaviours, while girls are more likely to internalise it.

Post-traumatic stress does not always present quietly. For many, especially boys, it shows up through anger, withdrawal, impulsivity, or risk-taking. These responses are often labelled as mental health or behavioural issues rooted in active risk and ongoing trauma. Without safety and support, they often escalate into criminal activity and conduct with lifelong consequences. Without safe spaces, consistent support, and adults who understand trauma, these responses escalate rather than settle. What begins as distress becomes behaviour. What becomes behaviour is punished. And once punishment replaces support, harm compounds.

Research also shows that boys are less likely to access early emotional support, particularly where there are limited safe spaces, limited education around emotional literacy, and a lack of healthy role models.

Long-term studies are clear. Childhood trauma that is unsupported does not disappear with age. It carries forward. These children become adults, and without change, generational patterns continue. Equality does not mean taking safety away from girls. It means extending safety, stability, education, and support to boys as well. All children need protection, guidance, and care if we want different outcomes in the future.

We are on the right path. The silence has been broken. But the evidence shows we still have a long way to go to achieve real balance, real safety, and lasting generational healing.

I was already living inside what happens when that healing does not exist.

Miss a deadline, and it became evidence. Ask too many questions, and it became resistance. Advocate for your child, and it was called obstruction. I was constantly aware that my children's futures depended on how well I could perform coherence under pressure. There was no space to fall apart. Trauma was acknowledged in theory but punished in practice.

I have been called crazy, and there have been repeated attempts to silence me by individuals and institutions that were uncomfortable with my truth. I am not crazy. I am not stupid. And, unfortunately for them, I was not on drugs. What I experienced was not personal failure. It was systemic failure. And naming that is not bitterness. It is clarity.

I Love Me Anyway is a four week in person and online offering for people who want to love themselves a little more and gather tools to carry through life. We move with the moon cycles, breathe, journal, and work with sound, crystals, and oils, building simple rituals and a personal toolkit to stay grounded and present. Not by ignoring what happened, but by learning to be with ourselves anyway.

When I Love Me Anyway was first offered in person, it filled easily. People returned each week, brought journals already marked and folded, and spoke about small shifts that were beginning to ripple outward. The sessions were gentle by design. Breathing. Reflection. Sound. Simple ritual. But the effects were not small.

Again and again, people spoke about doing something radical for the first time. Listening to themselves without immediately overriding their own needs.

What I had not expected was how quickly the work began to move beyond the room.

At the time, I was regularly asked whether I would take the work online. I did not. I was still too nervous to be visible in that way.

I did not yet trust that my voice could exist safely in public space. So the work stayed contained. In rooms. Among people who had chosen to be there.

One woman, a school teacher, attended only the first session. I noticed her absence in the following weeks but did not question it. Many months later, at a Reiki practice day, she approached me. She apologised for not returning and then explained why. The first session had given her something she had not realised she was missing. Permission. She told me she went home and decided to love herself anyway.

That decision set difficult changes in motion. She shared that leaving her marriage came with serious consequences, including hospitalisation and court involvement. What she wanted me to know was this. She was still out. She was still safe. And she was still teaching. She told me she carried the message of self-worth into her classroom, sharing with her students that loving yourself is not selfish, and that choosing yourself does not require perfection. She was proud, not because everything had resolved neatly, but because she had not abandoned herself.

Another participant came to the work carrying a different struggle. She was navigating her relationship with her adult son and felt she had lost autonomy over decisions about her own life, including where she would live. Over the four week period, she began using the tools we practised. Journalling. Grounding. Boundary awareness. Slowly, she shifted from asking for permission to listening inwardly. By the end of the sessions, she had taken steps to move to a place that felt right to her, creating clearer and healthier boundaries with her son in the process. The change was not dramatic on the surface. It was foundational.

These moments mattered to me because they reflected the true intention of the work. I Love Me Anyway was never about fixing people or pushing them toward a particular outcome. It was about restoring relationship. With the self. With intuition. With choice.

At the time, choosing not to take the work online was about safety. Mine and my children's. Visibility carries risk, especially for women who have already been misread, mislabelled, and punished for speaking. Staying offline allowed the work to remain contained and relational. It meant I could hold space without having to defend my credibility or explain my pain to strangers.

But the world has changed. Or perhaps it has simply revealed itself more clearly.

What I see now is not an isolated need, or a niche audience. I see families everywhere struggling with the same core wounds. Disconnection from self. Fear of speaking up. Blurred boundaries mistaken for love. Compliance mistaken for safety. Children learning early that their feelings are inconvenient, that silence is rewarded, and that endurance is a virtue even when it hurts.

There is a worldwide need for self-love, self-advocacy, and boundaries. Not as concepts, but as lived skills. Families and children do not need systems that seek to control, fragment, or punish them. They need systems that support, assist, and stabilise.

Too many stories begin as fairytales. Promises of protection. Of love. Of happily ever after. When those fairytales fracture, what follows is often confusion and shame. The narrative shifts quietly from hope to endurance. From endurance to survival. And for too many families, survival turns into something unrecognisable. Nightmares. Then real-life horror stories, not because people failed, but because support arrived too late, or not at all.

I am willing to be visible now because silence does not serve this moment. The work of loving yourself anyway is no longer optional or indulgent. It is foundational. When people learn to recognise their own worth, to name their needs, and to hold boundaries with compassion, the ripple effects move outward. Into families. Into classrooms. Into communities. Into the way children learn what is normal and what is not.

I am still careful. I am still protective. But I am no longer willing to stay small when the need is this widespread. The work has shown me, again and again, that when people are given permission to listen to themselves, they do not become reckless. They become grounded. They do not abandon responsibility. They reclaim it.

This is why I am willing to take the work forward now. Not because everything is resolved, but because the cost of staying silent is too high. Loving yourself anyway is not about bypassing pain or pretending harm did not happen. It is about refusing to disappear inside it. It is about choosing presence, choice, and dignity, even in imperfect conditions. Especially then.

And I Love Me Anyway was not born from collapse. It was born from remembering who I was when everything tried to erase me. We are only at the very start of our healing journey, and it is coming despite still not having safety from the legal system. I have just become a published author in this book and am beginning my own writing, creating a Guidance oracle deck, and running personal and group classes. I am focused on healing my relationship with my children and myself, working with both human and spiritual systems, and providing spiritual tools and support. I continue to tell my story and push for change that allows real safety and generational healing. I am starting again from zero. Even small beginnings carry their own kind of magic, capable of unfolding into waves of change, and this is the first ripple I cast as I walk this path, step by step.

What comes next is not an ending. It is ongoing.

I am not working toward a neat outcome. I am working toward stability. Toward lives that are calm enough for nervous systems to settle. Toward children who are allowed to be children, and supported to develop the skills to manage their world. Toward adults who are learning that their needs do not make them difficult.

I am interested in what happens when safety is built slowly, not demanded through compliance. When healing is allowed to take time. When listening to yourself is not treated as a problem.

The work ahead is practical. It is about boundaries. About choice. About giving people tools they can actually use when systems are confusing, slow, or unsafe. It is not about fixing anyone. It is about reducing harm.

For me, this means continuing to write, to teach, and to offer this work in ways that are careful and grounded. It means focusing on my children and our relationship. It means staying present, even when disappearing would be easier.

I do not know exactly where this leads. I do know why it matters. Small steps count. They accumulate. And they move us toward systems that support rather than add to cumulative trauma.

My mission is to give every person I come in contact with permission to love themselves anyway, even when it feels hard.

Especially when it feels hard.

This chapter reflects my lived experience and personal perspective. It does not purport to represent legal findings or identify individuals or organisations.

"Don't cry to quit. Cry to keep going!"

~ Eric Thomas

About the Author

Catherine Parkes is a mother, spiritual healing advisor, Reiki Master, and the creator of I Love Me Anyway. Her work is informed by lived experience and formal qualifications, including many years working as an aged care nurse, which shaped her trauma-informed, people-centred approach to healing and self-leadership. Catherine is known for her direct, emotionally honest way of speaking, giving voice to experiences often left unspoken and creating space for truth, accountability, and change.

Alongside her professional work, Catherine advocates for family law and domestic violence systems to adopt trauma-informed, child-focused frameworks that prioritise safety and access to wraparound services to support family healing and child safety reform. Outside her work, Catherine finds peace in and around water and enjoys play, camping, and outdoor activities with her children, with a focus on generational healing and holding space for love, reconnection, and return.

Email: connect@ilovemeanyway.com

Facebook: www.facebook.com/ilovemeanywaycathparkes

Website: www.ilovemeanyway.com

Kathryn Rands

What if the moment your life shattered was the moment your soul began to awaken?

I believed awakening arrived quietly —moments of stillness, clarity, or peace. Not betrayal, loss, and slow unravelling of everything I thought was secure. Yet it was in the breaking that my true journey began. What felt like devastation was in truth the stripping away of the life I had outgrown so that something deeper, wiser, and more aligned could finally emerge.I never imagined that my life would one day become a story. At least, not the kind people would want to read. Stories I believed were for the brave and extraordinary. I didn't feel like any of those. Just a woman trying to breathe without collapsing under everything I carried.

But sometimes, life writes you into a story you never chose — and you survive it anyway.

And that survival becomes your voice.

This is mine.......

'How much more alone can you be?'

These words gave me the wake-up call I so desperately needed.

Growing up I never appreciated how lucky I was with loving parents and a beautiful stable environment. But I did know I wanted what my mum and dad had, true happiness.

So, when I married and had two children, I thought it would be forever.

However, a business from success to disaster changed him.

His personality changed beyond recognition as he worked away. Meanwhile I kept the business afloat with dad, alongside work, two children, a home and caring for mum with Leukaemia. I was faced daily with debt collectors while his head was buried in the sand.

Enough was enough!

I challenged him but wished I hadn't!

The word affair as my world fell apart; my thoughts immediately of protecting my girls, eight and four, so agreed everything would continue and sorted after Christmas.

Nothing changed, he was still doing as he pleased.

Deep down I knew **I** was the one with my head in the sand!!!

A friend listened attentively and questioned my fears. My actual words were 'I can't do this on my own'.

Her reply hit like a bolt of lightening…

HOW MUCH MORE ALONE CAN YOU BE ?!?!!!!!!!!!!!!!

Everyone could see I was already doing everything but my fears of responsibility for children alone had always felt beyond my limits but I now had no choice!!

Christmas Eve, I found myself filing for divorce while he was with her.

But I realised although the ground may give way —

you can learn to build on the ruins,

and you can rise stronger than you ever believed possible.

The affair didn't just end a marriage — it triggered a chain reaction. From being a wife and mother, to standing in the ruins of divorce papers, business debt, bailiffs, no maintenance and two children needing stability with a future that felt painfully uncertain.

The ultimate insult, waving my girls off in his new car with a woman playing happy families, while I fought to survive emotionally and financially.

Anti-depressants became a lifeline as I tried to remember who I was beneath the pain.

But here's the truth no one tells you:

Even when everything falls apart, there is a part of you — however small — that refuses to die.

For a long time, mine was just a flicker. A flame hidden beneath exhaustion and the endless to-do lists of a single mother trying to survive. But flickers have a way of growing when you give them the slightest breath of hope.

Slowly, painfully, I began to rebuild. Not because I was brave, but because I had no choice.

But transformation rarely announces itself.

It happens quietly while you think you're just surviving and then eventually, I was strengthening and finding myself beneath the rubble.

The woman I found was different.

She was stronger than the one who had been betrayed.

She was more compassionate than her who had once tried to hold everything together alone.

She had discovered that pain can become purpose if you're willing to turn and face it.

From that point, healing didn't feel like an impossibility — it felt like an invitation.

I prayed my girls' lives would be gentler than mine had been. But the universe has its own curriculum, and sometimes our children walk paths we would do anything to shield them from.

My daughter, bright and sensitive, entered a relationship that slowly became a fifteen-year storm. It was controlling, draining, emotionally corrosive. Like many toxic relationships, it tightened gradually, until leaving felt impossible. I watched her change. Her confidence faded. Her voice softened. Her light dimmed. I stayed close without pushing — aware that judgement would only isolate her further. This was my first lesson in what it truly means to guide rather than rescue.

As a mother, I felt the same helplessness I'd once felt standing in front of the bailiffs—frightened, grieving, desperate to protect what mattered most.

I knew she was fighting a battle no one could fight for her. I wanted to rescue her, to shout at the universe for letting her suffer. But healing cannot be forced; only supported. I never confronted him to lose my daughter so I always kept the peace.

However, the reality of supporting an adult child who is still emotionally trapped was exhausting. I reminded her who she was when she forgot. I became her anchor in a world that kept trying to pull her under.

And then came the moment that changed us both forever.

I would be lying if I said I was happy with her pregnancy. I knew she would probably be tied to him forever. I felt angry, helpless and lost.

But as I watched her preparing to become a mother, I knew I would be there to cherish this baby…

But some chapters in life are written with tears before they're written with words.

The day she lost the baby…was the day time stopped. The world moved, but we didn't. The air shifted, but we couldn't breathe. I held my daughter as she sobbed from a place no mother should ever have to witness—a place beyond grief, beyond pain, beyond comprehension.

There is no spiritual bypass for that kind of loss.

No affirmations strong enough.

No teachings wise enough.

No mother strong enough to fix it.

All I could do was hold her.

Hold her and pray.

Pray for her heart.

Pray for her spirit.

Pray that one day she would rise again.

We learned grief and silence together.

We learned that sometimes survival is the only goal for a while.

And in that sacred stillness, I realised something:

Motherhood isn't just raising children.

It is raising souls.

And sometimes it is holding a soul through darkness until it finds its own light again.

As the baby's gender could not be determined, my daughter chose a boy's name — the only certainty available in a moment of unbearable uncertainty. Christened on the same day as the funeral, a sacred blending of welcome and farewell, love and loss held in the same breath.

Later, the post-mortem revealed what we never expected: the baby was a girl.

The truth didn't undo the love or the naming; it simply deepened it.

She had already been known, blessed, and mourned — not by gender, but by soul.

I would carry forever, the soul is not bound by names or certainty. She came, she was loved, and she left having already changed us. From that place of unbearable grief, my role shifted once again — not to fix the pain, but to hold my daughter steady while she learned how to breathe through it.

However, she lived with an absence that felt impossible to carry. Still within the same relationship, she went on to have another child — not from certainty, but from a deep and human longing to restore meaning after loss.

Her son was later diagnosed with autism and global developmental delay. Parenting quickly became complex, demanding constant adjustment, advocacy, and emotional resilience. The weight of responsibility was heavy, and the future uncertain.

Throughout this time, my role remained consistent. I did not step in to direct or resolve, but to remain present. I supported and stayed grounded when things felt overwhelming. I learned that guidance is not about leading the way — it is about steadiness, patience, and trusting another person's capacity to find their own footing.

My experiences — of breakdown, rebuilding, and long-term emotional holding — led me on a journey to truly find myself because I understood what it feels like sitting inside uncertainty and continuing breathing anyway.

I am spiritual and accepted God and the Universe had a plan. Survival gradually became my purpose.

I trained in Reiki, Meditation, EFT, Qi Gong Vitality Coach and NLP Masters Practitioner.

I do not lead from a place of having overcome everything but from a place of having remained. Those I help do not need fixing. They need space, steadiness, and permission to move at their own pace.

I run mini retreats for groups whereby people relax, recharge and reset, also provide 1-1, all offered by Zoom too.

One of my clients had lost her husband sixteen years previously and had also lost herself with grief and anxiety , not having been to the hairdressers in years.

After her second session she messaged me from the hairdressers and said. 'I have found myself again'.

Another client who now comes regularly to my sessions was suffering from fibromyalgia and was riddled with pain. However, after only one session, she left trouble free.

Ultimately, my daughter entrusted my help and attends regularly and I continue supporting her, not as the rescuer but as a grounded, spiritually aligned mother walking beside her — strong, centred, whole.

And in watching her rise, I understood the deeper purpose of my own painful journey:

I wasn't just healing myself.

I was learning how to guide others through their darkness — my daughter included because I know firsthand that darkness is not an enemy — it is the doorway.

My purpose is no longer something I search for; it is something I embody.

When I began writing, I believed I was documenting a completed chapter of resilience — something already understood, lived through. I never anticipated that life would quietly place another threshold in front of me, asking for the same steadiness, patience, and presence from me.

For the past twenty-six years, my dad has been my constant after losing my mum, my confidant, my best friend. When everything felt unstable, he was the one place that remained reliable and calm.

For the last month I have not left his side being told he was nearing the end of his life.

The roles shifted. The man who once held everything steady now relied on my presence, my patience, and my willingness to simply be there. There was no fixing left to do. Only showing up, listening, and honouring the life that shaped mine.

The last things he said to me were simple and unwavering. He said he had always believed in me and whispered, ' love you angel and we won't be beat.' I treasure those words and keep going with steadiness and heart.

I understand more clearly that resilience is learning to rise with compassion for yourself when life has tried to break you. I entrusted God's help and my wonderful dad went to heaven on my beautiful mum's birthday which is so comforting.

I did not rise by escaping the fire — I rose through it.

***

Dad's Eulogy I read to him and so with his blessing….

Wherever I go dad, whatever I do, I want you to know dad this is for you.

Thank you for being such an incredible part of my life,
You taught me right from wrong and how to deal with strife.
No greater father could I have had; you were one of a kind
The greatest legacy untouchable that you have left behind.

I loved listening to your stories; they were the very best.
You were one of twelve kids, but more trouble than the rest.
You left home at sixteen, that's when your navy career began.
Women, cigs and beer each day, that's when you became a man

You were at sea for months on end, around the world, all countries to see.
Your stories always carried the theme that your happy place was by the sea.
You left the navy and met my mum, and the rest is history.
No sweeter couple in all the world could there ever be.

You did everything together and made the happiest home.
The best childhood a girl could have, I never needed to roam.
We spent time picking blackberries, strawberries and conkering too.
You built me a go-kart; there was nothing you couldn't do.

You took me swimming on a Sunday, taught me diving in the pool.
Patience, laughter and kindness, I didn't need to break the rules.
Pop and crisps in the pub gardens, at Yeadon we watched the planes.
Surprise view walks on Otley Chevin. It didn't matter if there was rain.

You taught me how to ride a bike, play cards and not to cheat.
You gave me strength and independence to stand on my own two feet.
You took me out for driving lessons and showed me how to check my car.
You taught me not to live in debt and said with that I would go far.

You were an electrician by trade but were much more than that.
Plumbing, building ,DIY, you could wear just any hat.
Your work ethic was second to none, Evenings and weekends as well as days.
You were a great provider but taught me how to pay my way.

You paid for my weddings and walked me down the aisle.

You helped me with my first house, always went the extra mile.

You took my dog out daily, helped my business when it was failing.

I never paid you anything as I walked away with nothing.

Through all the sleepless nights I had, you cared when I was ill.

Wow dad what memories I have, you've left big boots to fill.

The saddest day of all our lives was the day mum passed away.

You carried on beyond belief, with our help along the way.

You spent twenty years living alone, enjoyed time in your garden doing flowerpots.

Your passion was travelling on buses and trains and eating outside when hot.

You loved listening to music, CDs, DVDs and Alexa too.

Daniel O'Donnel, Forster and Allen were the ones for you.

Your happiest times were spent with us. Best dad, grandad and great grandad too.

You made the most magical games. Nothing too much trouble for you.

Using your stick, when being in goal, Playing dominoes, jigsaws and water bombs

You mesmerised us when struggling to see but playing keyboard and knowing our songs.

You loved to come away with us, or just to go out for tea.

A little walk around the park. Your favourite, a house by the
sea.

You moved into The Borrins but came out much more than
most.

Usually to ours for scampi and chips, or soup or a Sunday
roast.

You loved us unconditionally; with a patience no-one can
touch.

A special place always in our hearts, we love you so very much.

I could go on forever sharing all the memories we have.

You are and always will be, our superhero dad and grandad.

We will never be ready to let you go, but our loss is Heaven's
gain.

Mum has waited twenty-six years for you; it's time to be
together again.

But …. You always knew my thoughts dad, that this is not the
end.

Although our hearts are broken, I know we will see you again.

Thank you, we love you, you were one of a kind

It's time to be with mum again……until next time.

Wherever we go dad, whatever we do. Everything we all are
today is because of mum and you.

Goodnight….. God Bless xx

***

My life has taught me that resilience isn't loud or perfect — it's the quiet courage to keep going when your heart feels heavy and the path feels uncertain. Healing doesn't erase what you've lived through; it transforms it into strength, compassion, and purpose. Holding my dad's hand as he took his last breath changed me forever — it ignited a flame that will never extinguish. I now hold space for others because I've learned how to hold myself.

I learned the truth I now teach others:

You are never being ruined.

You are always being redirected.

You are always being reborn.

For the last twenty- seven years my wonderful husband has stood beside me as my best friend and trusted confidant — a man whose belief in me has never wavered. He consistently invested in me emotionally, practically, and financially, creating the stability, safety, and freedom that allowed me to grow, take courageous risks, and become everything I am today.

Together, we were blessed with a beautiful son, who gently blended our family together, uniting my two daughters and my husband's son into one connected, loving family. Family time reflects the strength, love, and resilience that ground everything we do.

My vision is to help others believe in themselves and understand there is always hope!!!

Your past does not determine your future...

My story didn't break me.

It built me into someone stronger and wiser because I've lived every chapter of the struggle myself.

It became my strength and my service to others.

This isn't a story about pain.

It is about rising.

About standing in the ashes of a life you didn't choose and deciding to create something better.

Step by step, I rebuilt not just my life, but my identity...

And now, my voice exists for one reason:

To remind others that no matter how heavy life feels — you can rise, you can rebuild, and you can shine again and we are not defined by adversity, but by who we choose to become afterwards.

No matter what you've survived, your light is still alive. It is always Time2shine.

My motto is 'If I can, you can'; The question is ………. CAN YOU?

About the Author

Kathryn is the founder of Time2shine UK, an NLP Master Practitioner /holistic therapist dedicated to helping people release stress, anxiety, grief, emotional blocks to connect with their true selves. She supports individuals feeling overwhelmed, stuck / disconnected to regain clarity, confidence and emotional freedom.

Her approach blends powerful NLP techniques, Timeline Therapy, Reiki, Breathwork, EFT Tapping and Meditation, creating a deeply supportive and results-driven healing experience through 1:1 sessions, mini retreats and transformational programmes.

Kathryn's compassion is strengthened by her previous work supporting the mental health charity Mind, alongside her personal fundraising challenge of running every day to raise awareness and funds. These experiences reflect her belief in resilience, consistency and wellbeing.

Outside her professional work, Kathryn treasures time with her family and three grandsons, who continually remind her of joy, presence and purpose. Her mission is simple — helping others feel lighter, calmer, ready to shine from the inside out.

Email: time2shine63@outlook.com

Facebook: www.facebook.com/Kathryn.Rands

Website: www.time-2-shine-baildon.co.uk

Alyson Richelle

What I Didn't Know Then (And What I Know Now)

Two years ago, I shared my story publicly for the first time.

At the time, I thought I understood what I was writing about. I believed I was telling the truth, and I was. But I didn't yet understand how incomplete that truth still was. Not because I was dishonest, but because awareness often arrives long before understanding does.

Back then, I was beginning to wake up.
Now, I understand what it actually takes to stay awake.

This chapter is not a rewrite because the original story was wrong. It's a rewrite because growth has layers. Survival teaches you how to endure. Healing teaches you how to choose. Implementation is a very different thing to insight.

What I didn't know then is how much work would come after the realisation.

What I didn't know then is how lonely clarity can be.

What I didn't know then is that seeing the pattern is only the beginning. Living differently requires dismantling your entire internal operating system.

The Frog in the Pot

There's an analogy I come back to again and again now, because it explains so much of what people struggle to understand from the outside.

The frog in the pot.

If you drop a frog into boiling water, it jumps out immediately. The danger is obvious. The pain is instant. The threat is clear.

But if you place a frog in cool water and slowly turn up the heat, it stays. It adapts. It adjusts. The temperature rises so gradually that what would once have felt unbearable becomes normal.

Until it isn't survivable anymore.

This is how so many people find themselves trapped in unhealthy relationships, systems, workplaces, and identities. Not because they are weak. Not because they lack intelligence. Adaptation is a survival skill, and survival does not require clarity. It requires endurance.

When something becomes your normal, you stop questioning it.

You stop measuring it against what you deserve. You stop trusting the part of yourself that whispers, something isn't right here.

By the time the pain becomes visible to others, the person inside it has already been living in that heat for years.

Two years ago, I was still in the pot. I just didn't know it yet.

What makes the frog-in-the-pot analogy so confronting is not just the slow rise in temperature. It's how convincingly the water feels normal while it's happening.

At first, nothing feels wrong. The compromises are small. The explanations sound reasonable. You tell yourself you're overthinking. You adjust your expectations, then adjust them again. You stop asking whether something is healthy and start asking whether you're just being difficult.

Self-doubt doesn't arrive as a loud alarm. It arrives quietly, disguised as logic. Maybe I'm too sensitive. Maybe I misunderstood. Maybe this is just how things are.

Over time, your internal reference point shifts. What once would have triggered concern now feels familiar. What once would have been unacceptable becomes tolerable. Because the change is gradual, you don't experience it as danger. You experience it as an adaptation.

This is where shame enters the picture.

When others finally notice the situation, the question is rarely "what happened to you?" It's "why did you stay?" The judgement does not land on the conditions that shaped the behaviour, but instead on the person who adapted to survive them.

That judgement compounds the harm. It reinforces silence. It teaches people to question their own perceptions rather than the environment they were responding to. It keeps people stuck in the pot long after the water has become unsafe.

Understanding this has changed how I view my past, and how I respond to others now. Staying wasn't a moral failure. It was a survival response. Survival does not require clarity. It requires endurance.

Once you see that, the narrative shifts. The shame loosens. And the possibility of change becomes real. Not because someone else demanded it, but because you finally trust yourself enough to notice the heat.

Awareness Is Not the Same as Freedom

When I wrote my original chapter, I had begun to recognise patterns. I could see behaviours for what they were. I could name things that had once felt confusing or shameful.

What I didn't yet understand was that naming something does not automatically free you from it.

Awareness without boundaries becomes self-betrayal.
Insight without action becomes another form of paralysis.

At that point, I was still trying to please people who benefitted from my silence. Still explaining myself to people who had no intention of understanding me. Still hoping that if I communicated better, tried harder, stayed softer, things would change.

I didn't yet realise that clarity often makes others uncomfortable, especially those invested in you staying small, compliant, or available.

Growth isn't just about learning new things. It's about unlearning the strategies that once kept you safe but now keep you stuck.

And that process is rarely celebrated.

What I Didn't Understand Then

When I first shared my story, I had insight, but I didn't yet have capacity.

I could see patterns, but I didn't understand what it would cost to live differently. Awareness alone doesn't dismantle conditioning. It exposes it.

I didn't know how much energy it would take to hold boundaries consistently. How often I would second-guess myself. How many times I'd be tempted to soften my truth just to avoid conflict or discomfort?

I didn't understand how many people would fall away once I stopped performing the version of myself they were comfortable with. I didn't understand that some connections were sustained not by mutual respect, but by my willingness to over-function.

Most of all, I didn't understand how much self-trust I would need to build. Slowly, deliberately, and without external validation.

Insight gave me language. Implementation demanded courage.

Looking back now, I can see I wasn't failing to change. I was learning how. I was building the internal strength required to tolerate discomfort without abandoning myself.

Growth doesn't happen all at once. It unfolds in stages. This stage, the one between realisation and embodiment, is the least visible and the least supported.

But it's also where real transformation begins.

When Intensity Isn't Intimacy

One of the patterns I didn't fully understand then, but see clearly now, is how quickly relationships can form when intensity is mistaken for connection.

Love bombing doesn't arrive as danger. It arrives as relief.

It feels like being seen. Like being chosen. Like finally being understood after a long period of uncertainty or pain. The pace feels flattering, even reassuring, especially when you've been starved of safety or consistency.

But intensity is not intimacy.

Real intimacy unfolds slowly. It respects pacing. It allows discernment. It leaves room for choice.

When connection accelerates too quickly, it can bypass consent. Not overtly, but emotionally. Before you realise it, expectations form, roles solidify, and boundaries feel harder to introduce without consequence.

What I didn't know then is that fast attachment can be a warning sign. Not of passion, but of unspoken agendas. Of needs seeking fulfilment rather than mutuality seeking growth.

Once I learned to slow down, to notice how my body responded rather than how convincing words sounded, everything shifted.

And not everyone appreciated that shift.

The Cost of Cutting Ties

One of the hardest lessons I've had to learn over the last year is that not everyone can come with you.

This sounds simple. It isn't.

We're taught, explicitly and implicitly, that loyalty means endurance. That compassion means self-sacrifice. That boundaries are selfish. That saying no is rude. That prioritising yourself is abandonment.

Layered over that is guilt conditioning. The belief that if someone is upset by your boundary, you must have done something wrong. That their discomfort is your responsibility to fix.

For a long time, I stayed agreeable not because I wanted to, but because I was afraid of what would happen if I didn't. Afraid of being alone. Afraid of not coping. Afraid of losing connection altogether.

People-pleasing can feel like safety when you've learned that relationships are conditional.

Choosing myself meant losing people. Not suddenly, but quietly. Invitations stopped. Support thinned. Dynamics shifted. Not because I became cruel or uncaring, but because I stopped absorbing what was never mine to carry.

What surprised me most wasn't the loss itself. It was the relief that followed.

The quiet.
The steadiness.
The absence of constant self-monitoring.

Loneliness, I learned, is not the same as isolation. Being surrounded by people who don't see you, don't respect your boundaries, or don't want you to change is one of the loneliest experiences there is.

Letting go wasn't cruelty.
It was honesty.
And it was necessary.

When Boundaries Trigger Escalation

This was something I didn't expect.

I believed, naively, that setting boundaries would create distance, not danger. That clarity would bring resolution, not escalation.

What I didn't understand is how quickly dynamics can shift when you stop being compliant.

When you no longer play your assigned role, some people don't simply walk away. They react. They reframe. They resist. They attempt to regain control, sometimes overtly, sometimes strategically.

Support can turn conditional. Narratives can change. Your character can be questioned. Your credibility can be undermined.

Safety, emotional, psychological, sometimes physical, can suddenly feel fragile.

This is one of the reasons people stay quiet.

It's not fear of leaving. It's the fear of what comes after.

Reason, Season, or Lifetime

People come into our lives for a reason, a season, or a lifetime.

I used to cling to the idea that everyone was meant to stay. That if a relationship ended, it meant I had failed. That endings were something to fix or avoid.

Now I understand that some people are mirrors. Some are teachers. Some are companions. Some are chapters, not conclusions.

The mistake I made for years was trying to turn seasons into lifetimes.

Growth requires revisiting who came into your life, why they came, and what role they played. Not to assign blame, but to reclaim agency.

Some people showed me what love isn't.

Some showed me how easily care can become control.

Some showed me my own patterns, my tolerance, my fear of conflict, my habit of over-functioning.

And some showed me the strength I didn't know I had, simply by leaving.

Self-Trust: The Forgotten Skill

If there is one thing I wish I could go back and tell the version of myself who wrote that first chapter, it's this.

You are the one constant in your life.

Through every relationship. Every friendship. Every system. Every role you inhabit. You are the common denominator. Not as a source of blame, but as a source of power.

We're conditioned to outsource our authority. To trust experts over instincts. To defer to systems over self. To doubt our perceptions if they make others uncomfortable.

Relearning self-trust has been one of the most uncomfortable and necessary processes of my life.

It meant listening to my body when my mind tried to override it.
It meant honouring my no without justifying it.
It meant accepting that clarity does not require consensus.

Self-trust doesn't make life easier. It makes it truer.

It's tempting to focus entirely on what others did wrong.

Blame can feel grounding. It offers a clear direction for anger and a sense of moral clarity. Sometimes it's warranted.

But blame alone doesn't restore agency.

The harder, and ultimately more empowering, work is turning inward without turning against yourself. Asking not "what's wrong with me?" but "what did I learn to tolerate, and why?"

Responsibility, in this sense, is not about fault. It's about choice. It's about recognising that while we cannot control what happened to us, we can influence what happens next.

Self-trust is rebuilt through action, not affirmation. Through small decisions that honour your internal signals. Through saying no once, then again, then again, until your nervous system begins to believe you will protect yourself.

This is how safety is rebuilt from the inside out.

When you trust yourself, you no longer need constant reassurance from others. You don't need agreement to validate your experience. You don't need permission to act in your own best interests.

You become less reactive, not because you care less, but because you are no longer outsourcing your sense of stability.

That shift changes everything. Not overnight, but irreversibly.

When Systems Respond to Self-Protection

Another hard truth I've had to face is that systems don't always respond well to people who stop complying quietly.

Following instructions does not guarantee protection. Reporting concerns does not guarantee support. Speaking up does not guarantee safety.

In some cases, it does the opposite.

I learned how quickly credibility can be questioned when you persist. How easily concern can be reframed as a nuisance. How exhausting it is to be repeatedly scrutinised while simply trying to keep yourself and your children safe.

Long hours of questioning. Delays. Silence. Being reframed as "difficult" rather than at risk.

This experience reshaped my understanding of why so many people disengage. Not because they don't care, but because the emotional cost of engagement becomes unsustainable.

The Slow Work of Implementation

What people don't talk about is how long it takes to live differently after you wake up.

There is grief in growth. Grief for the time lost. The versions of yourself you abandoned. The boundaries you didn't yet know how to hold.

There is also exhaustion. Because unlearning is labour. Unlike survival, healing doesn't run on adrenaline.

I had to stop asking, "Why am I like this?"
And start asking, "What did this protect me from once?"

I had to accept that some patterns don't disappear. They require daily management. Conscious choice. Repetition.

Growth is not a breakthrough moment. It's a thousand small decisions made when no one is watching.

Safety, Stability, and the Cost of Uncertainty

There is nothing theoretical about safety.

It is housing.
It is predictability.
It is being able to rest.

Periods of instability, including displacement and uncertainty, strip people back to survival mode. When you are focused on securing basic stability, healing becomes secondary. Not because it isn't important, but because safety comes first.

This is another reason simplistic advice does harm.

You cannot heal in chaos.
You cannot reflect while bracing.
You cannot rebuild while constantly searching for ground to stand on.

Understanding this changed how I measure strength, both in myself and in others.

I didn't fully understand then that instability doesn't just disrupt your schedule. It disrupts your sense of self. When you're living in uncertainty, your nervous system doesn't file it as a tough season. It files it as a threat.

In that state, even simple decisions feel heavy. You lose access to the version of you that plans, creates, and thinks long-term. You become a person who is scanning, managing, and bracing. Then people misread that as being too much, too emotional, or not coping.

But coping isn't proof of safety. It's proof of adaptation.

What changed for me was recognising that stability is not a luxury. It's a foundation. It's what allows you to think clearly, hold boundaries, and rebuild without constantly being pulled back into survival. That understanding made me gentler with myself, and far less willing to minimise what safety actually requires.

Choosing Responsibility Without Shame

There is a difference between responsibility and blame.

Blame keeps you stuck. Responsibility gives you leverage.

For a long time, I oscillated between self-blame and external blame. Neither led to change. What finally shifted things was taking responsibility for my patterns without shaming myself for developing them.

I didn't cause what happened to me.
But I am responsible for what I do with it now.

That distinction changed everything.

It allowed me to step out of victimhood without denying harm. To honour survival without staying defined by it. To choose growth without pretending it was easy.

From Story to Service

What I didn't foresee when I first shared my story was how many people would recognise themselves in it.

Not just survivors, but professionals. Parents. Advocates. People are quietly questioning their own normal.

That's when What They Don't Tell You stopped being a concept and became a responsibility.

Because once you see the pattern, you can't unsee it. Once you understand how invisible harm works, silence becomes a form of complicity.

This work isn't about saving anyone. It's about giving language to what so many feel but can't yet articulate.

It's about bridging the gap between awareness and action. Between knowing something is wrong and knowing what to do next.

Standing Alone to Stand Strong

I won't pretend this journey has been graceful. Or linear. Or clean.

There have been moments of doubt. Of grief. Of wanting to retreat into familiarity because growth was too quiet, too slow, too lonely.

But what I know now, without hesitation, is that choosing myself did not diminish me. It returned me to myself.

I am not the same person who wrote that first chapter. I am deeply proud of her for starting.

This version of me exists because she asked the questions. Because she told the truth before she fully understood it. Because she took the first step.

And now, I continue. Not because I have all the answers, but because I trust myself enough to keep asking better questions.

If You See Yourself Here

If any part of this story feels familiar, I want you to know this.

You are not weak for adapting.
You are not broken for staying.
And you are not failing because change is slow.

You don't need to burn your life down to rebuild it. You need honesty, support, and time.

Most of all, you need permission from yourself to believe that your experience is valid, even if others don't understand it yet.

Growth doesn't announce itself.
It whispers.
And then, one day, you realise you're no longer willing to stay in water that's slowly boiling.

And that's when everything changes.

This work is not about perfection or arriving at some final version of yourself. It's about staying present, staying honest, and choosing, again and again, not to abandon yourself when things get uncomfortable.

I see you.
I believe you.
You aren't alone.

About the Author

Alyson Richelle is a trauma-informed educator, advocate, and systems navigator, and the founder of *What They Don't Tell You*. A former Senior Sergeant of Police with 15 years' service, Alyson brings a rare dual perspective as both a professional insider and a lived-experience survivor of trauma, coercive control, and systemic failure.

Her work focuses on bridging the gap between awareness and implementation. Helping people recognise hidden patterns of harm, rebuild self-trust, set boundaries, and navigate complex systems with clarity and confidence. Alyson supports survivors, parents, and professionals through education, mentoring, advocacy, and practical tools grounded in real-world experience.

Known for her honest, grounded approach, Alyson challenges silence, judgment, and oversimplified narratives around abuse and recovery. Her mission is to ensure people have the language, insight, and support they need to break cycles, reclaim agency, and create lasting change; for themselves and future generations.

Website: Www.wtdty.com.au

Email: Hello.alysonrichelle@gmail.com

Facebook: www.facebook.com/nosyla

Tracy Sedman

People tell the story differently. Some tell it like an urban myth that happened years ago. It has been told so many times that it no longer belongs to the woman at its centre. It has been shaped by repetition, distance, and the comfort of assumptions and believing the version spoken first — and loudest.

Some say she was heartbroken. She wanted to end her life.

Others say she was reckless. She had lost her mind.

There is one version that gets repeated more than the others.

In that version, she was — *and still is* — crazy.

That story comes from the same voice.

The storyteller.

The one who insists she always imagined things;

Who told her she did things, she knows she didn't do.
The one who says her river swim proves she is crazy.

That voice tells the story with certainty — a warning, a concern, a bullet dodged.

The details shift depending on the audience, but the conclusion never changes: *she's crazy*.

Because once she is labelled unstable, then nothing she says needs to be heard.

If she was out of touch with reality, then reality can be rewritten without her resistance.

They say she jumped from the jetty, into the black outgoing current. They say she wanted to die.

But others say she swam. That part unsettles the storyteller. It doesn't fit neatly with madness. A woman swimming with intention in the middle of the night disrupts a story built on instability. So, the emphasis returns to the label: *crazy*. That's how the storyteller finishes her story: how final it was meant to be.

But the river didn't take her.

And that, perhaps, is the part no one expected.

She survived.

And survival has a way of undoing a carefully constructed narrative.

She remained.

He had been her storyteller for too long.

She spoke.

The night I jumped into the river, I wasn't trying to die.

I didn't lose my mind because I was weak.
I lost it because I had been taught — slowly, deliberately — I couldn't trust myself.

I didn't lose my mind all at once.
I lost it in pieces, each time I ignored *my gut feelings, my instincts, my knowing*: because someone else insisted I was wrong.

By the time I stood in the rain that night, staring into a dangerous river, my body understood something my mind had been denying - staying inside someone else's version of reality was costing my identity, my well-being, and *could ultimately cost me my life.*

I was afraid — afraid of being controlled into a version of reality that was never mine. I couldn't carry someone else's distortions anymore and abandon my reality altogether.

If you have ever been told, *"you are crazy,"* or *"that didn't happen,"* *"you imagine things,"* or **doubted yourself** - this story is for you. Not because it ends neatly, but because it tells the truth.

Society has taught us that when a woman breaks, she was already unstable. What it does not tell us is how much pressure it takes to break someone who had been holding everything together, silently.

I didn't leave my home because I wanted to disappear. I left because the one place that had always been my sanctuary no longer felt safe — and *I was terrified of what would happen if I stayed and learned to doubt myself there.*

I left my home that night because my sanctuary had been invaded.
My home had always been my safe place — my family's refuge. A warm, open house where laughter came easily and people could be themselves without performance or pretence. I had built it that way. Carefully. Intentionally.

It was where my nervous system softened.
Where my body knew it could rest.
And then it didn't.

Not because the walls changed —
but because something entered that did not belong there.

I felt his presence. Occupying space, he had no right to occupy.
His version of events seeping into the corners of my thoughts.

Control doesn't always arrive with force.
Sometimes it arrives as an atmosphere.
Staying felt like a slow death.
So I left.

I walked along the sand toward the far end of the beach, following the curve of the shoreline, keeping my eyes on the navigational lights.

Red.
Green.

They blinked steadily along the river. I followed them as I walked the beach, letting their rhythm orient me.

The rain was relentless as I reached the rocky outcrop. It was slippery, so I took off my shoes, placing them carefully on the sand. I climbed barefoot over the rocks, choosing where to enter the water. I took off my long pants, wrapped my phone in them and placed them carefully between rocks – I planned on coming back to get it.

I watched the lights again, counting.

One.
Two.
Three.

I stepped into the water letting my body acclimatise.

The first time I pushed off, I misjudged - my ribs striking a submerged rock, the breath was knocked out of me. I climbed back onto the rocks, sitting in the rain until my breathing returned. Voices came to me — people I knew and trusted. My family.

"You've got this".
"You can do this".
"We'll meet you on the other side".

When my body was ready again, I entered the water.

I wanted to swim to the other side.
I chose to enter the water.

I knew I could swim the distance.
And that part mattered.

The doubt about my capability had been planted — but it did not come with me into the river.

I reclaimed myself stroke by stroke.
Lights appeared around me —
small, shimmering points, twinkling as I moved through the water.
What I felt, more than anything, *was safety*.

I rolled onto my back swimming under the moon for a while, rain falling onto my face. I felt happiness — deep, simple happiness. Freedom. Connection to the water and to myself.

I rolled back over, focused on a navigational light and swam toward it.

Then the song came.
Lights will guide you home…
And I will try to fix you.
I sang and I swam.

I climbed onto the navigational marker I had focused on. My feet and hands were cut and bleeding, but I felt no pain. I waited, counted again, then dove back in to swim the final leg to my destination.

Lights will guide you home

And ignite your bones

And I will try to fix you.
I continued singing and swimming.

The twinkling lights returned. A boat passed close behind, missing me by a few metres. When I reached the far side and grabbed the jetty, something nudged my leg. A shadow moved toward me. This was the only moment I felt fear. I fought instinctively with fists and kicks, until it moved away. The lights returned, and with them, safety.

When I did leave the water, I removed my wet clothing to avoid hypothermia, leaving only my underwear pants. I picked up a boogie board to cover my bare breasts and walked toward the streetlights, still singing, *lights will guide you home… and I will try to fix you.*

I searched for the right light. I found it at a house. A man was in the garage. His voice was calm. I told him I was looking for somewhere safe. He returned with his wife and warm clothes. He drove me to the police station, and I let him speak for me. I felt safe enough to let him. I had reached my destination; I sat at the counter, put my head down and closed my eyes.

Not long after the ambulance arrived, the warm clothes the stranger had lent me were removed, and I was wrapped in a silver blanket to prevent hypothermia and placed into the ambulance.

I felt safe.

I fell asleep.

When I woke in the hospital, under Mental Health Schedule, I was known only as the woman who swam across the river. I became frightened. I refused to speak to the psychiatrists – afraid of being labelled crazy again. My family spoke to the doctors, and they insisted I was not crazy and this was out of character.

Later, I learned I had previously met the Police Officer who called the ambulance on an unrelated matter. He also spoke: *"this behaviour is out of character to the woman I had previously met."*

Those voices mattered — I was incoherent, confused, frightened. Thanks to those voices who spoke for me, the Schedule was lifted quickly.

I endured many medical tests including an extraordinarily painful lumbar puncture, my screams terrifying my family.

The diagnosis: a fear-induced acute psychotic break.

That language can sound frightening when stripped of context. This was not an illness that appeared out of nowhere. And it was not a defining condition.

That night, I didn't swim because I was heartbroken or seeking death. I swam because I was terrified of a man who had built his life on deception, manipulation, and control and was trying to dismantle my reality with precision.

In his attempts to silence me, rewrite history, and prevent me from pursuing monies he owed me, the storyteller applied for a Protection Order to stop me from speaking the truth. The Application contained more than eighteen fabrications — an inverted, non-existent reality. It told a story of me that neither I, nor anyone who knew me, could recognise.

Police served it on me at my home — my sanctuary. His mask was off. The smear campaign was real. Years of gaslighting and coercive control, followed by the confrontation with fabricated claims, and the realisation that this person had been capable of sustained deception and hostility, induced overwhelming fear and the collapse of my remaining sense of safety.

From a medical perspective, prolonged threat dysregulates the nervous system. Cortisol remains elevated. Sleep fragments.

Reality destabilises not because it is false, but because it is constantly contested. Eventually, the brain prioritises survival over coherence.

Recovery, for me, began with the need for explanation — not as an abstract academic or clinical exercise, but as a lifeline. I needed to understand how a woman capable of sustained postgraduate study, who had long relied on the clarity and reliability of her mind, could be pushed to the lowest margins of cognitive functioning and experience an acute psychotic episode under prolonged psychological threat.

I needed to know how that collapse was possible, what forces had bent me so far past my limits, and why my mind — once my greatest strength and anchor — had become the place where everything finally gave way. Those answers weren't about blame. They were the scaffolding I needed to rebuild myself with clarity instead of shame, confusion, or silence.

Much later, once my body had begun to recover and my mind had enough distance to reflect safely, I searched for an explanation for the lights I saw in the water. I found a scientific one: bioluminescence.

I had seen it many times before in the river. This explanation matters to me. Not because it replaces what I felt — but because it grounds it.

Those lights I believe, kept me safe from sharks and gave me the strength to swim across the outgoing tide. Understanding the science, didn't strip the moment of meaning. It gave it context. And context, not dismissal — is how truth survives intact.

The night I swam, those lights made me feel safe. As I moved through the water, singing, *"Lights will guide you home…And I will try to fix you."*

The lights were real.

They moved with my body.

And my nervous system responded to what it perceived as safety.

Both can be true at the same time.

Recovery is not linear. It doesn't happen overnight. It is not a race to the finish line. Recovery, for me, was never about returning to who I was before. It has been about learning how to live well with the injury I now carry.

Psychological injury leaves traces in the nervous system and stress responses.

Healing has meant managing those responses through boundaries, structure, support, and respect for my limits, not as weaknesses, but as signals. Part of that management includes ongoing treatment; for me, medication is one tool among many that keeps my nervous system regulated, no different from managing a chronic physical or neurological injury.

There was another pivotal moment in my recovery which has stayed with me — quieter, but just as important.

Weeks after the Protection Order was withdrawn, as the allegations could not be substantiated, I spoke with a police officer who I had never met before. In that conversation, I found myself doing what I had learned to do after years of not being believed: I spoke, then immediately reached for proof. Evidence. Something to justify what I was saying before it could be questioned. Something to support my reality.

He stopped me.
Not abruptly. Not unkindly.
He told me I needed to stop doing that — offering evidence to prove myself — and to simply state what I knew to be true. At the time, I didn't fully understand why he said it. But something in me paused.

Months later I realised what he had done.
He treated my words as sufficient.

For the first time in years, I stepped off the witness stand inside my own mind.

And in doing so, he gave me back something I didn't know I'd lost - permission to trust my own voice, my reality without defending it.

For people who've lived under gaslighting, the nervous system learns:

If I don't prove it, I won't be believed
If I don't have evidence ready, I'll lose credibility
If I pause, someone else will rewrite the story

So, the need to provide evidence becomes a shield, even when no one is attacking.

What the Police Officer was gently trying to interrupt was that reflex. Not because it was wrong, but because I no longer needed it in that moment.

People subjected to gaslighting and coercive control often learn to anticipate disbelief — instinctively offering proof to defend their reality.

I have since learned to be a trained interviewer, that behaviour signals hyper-justification, not deception. I wasn't trying to convince him — I was showing I had learned not to be believed. But evidence supports truth — it doesn't create it.

I didn't need to earn credibility in that conversation.
I already had it.

In his blunt, practical way, he was offering permission for me to stand in my statement without defending it.
He wasn't silencing me.

He was restoring authority to me.

That moment mattered more than he could have known. *Rebuilding trust in myself wasn't magical. It was structural.* After years of being forced to defend my own reality, something in me finally shifted. My internal trust, my authority over myself, the part the loudest voice had worked so hard to erode in me —began to return. And with it came a deep, overdue tiredness, the kind that arrives only when the fight-or-flight inside you finally pauses. I didn't resist.

This is a lesson I carry into my work — helping others move from proving themselves to simply being believed, starting with themselves.

This interaction with the Police Officer showed how one regulated interaction can begin to interrupt years of conditioning. It showed that systems that cause harm can also heal, one positive interaction at a time.

Recovery is a practice.
And it is entirely compatible with competence, leadership, happiness, and purpose.

I didn't tell this story to be understood. I told it so what happened to me could be useful to others. Because once you truly understand what coercive control, gaslighting, and psychological abuse do to the human nervous system, you can no longer pretend that policies, tick-box training, or after-the-fact responses are enough.

What broke me was *not* mental illness. It was prolonged exposure to psychological threat, compounded by systems that misread injury as instability and control as conflict. When I finally saw that clearly, I stopped framing my recovery as personal healing alone. I began to see it as a societal design problem.

I didn't want to create another trauma story.
I wanted the truth, the reality — on record. A correction. A foundation.

I have left no loose ends for others to twist.

I have honoured my body without mythologising it.

I have named harm without being consumed by it.

I have turned my lived experience into clarity, and clarity into purpose.

I tell this story not to explain myself — but to change outcomes. So what happened to me does not keep happening to women in silence.

I tell my story with courage and restraint. With honesty and intelligence. I didn't just survive the experience — I took authorship back from it, and that is what gives my work its power.

Today, I work at the intersection of lived experience, regulation, and prevention, translating psychological harm into evidence-informed sexual safety and coercive control frameworks that move organisations beyond compliance toward genuine prevention.

I work in sectors where the cost of failure is high and often hidden, translating what happens to people under psychological threat into language decision-makers and society can no longer ignore.

My work focuses on identifying early warning signs, understanding how power, fear, and silence operate within systems, and helping communities and workplaces move from reactive response to genuine prevention — particularly through better understanding domestic violence, coercive control, and mental health. At its core, this work is about building cultures where reality is not punished for being inconvenient, and where people are believed, supported, and protected before they break.

Alongside this, my coaching and leadership work centres on identity reconstruction after trauma — supporting women who were not "broken," but injured, to reclaim authorship of their lives.

The night I swam across the river does not make me who I am.
But it revealed something I no longer ignore:
Survival is not the opposite of competence. It's often the proof of it.

What defines me now is not the moment my nervous system overloaded — but what I built once clarity returned.

Language where there had been silence.
Frameworks where there had been confusion.
Advocacy where there had been shame.

The storyteller was later charged with another offence, convicted, and sentenced.

A Police AVO remains in force.

I reclaimed my reality. Then I professionalised it. Then I turned it outward.

So fewer people would have to reach breaking point before being believed.

This story is not here to sensationalise trauma.

It is here to change outcomes.
And that is the work I continue — deliberately, visibly, and without apology.

An Excerpt from, *"Not My Shame to Bear"* by Tracy Anne Sedman due for release late 2026

About the Author

Tracy Anne Sedman is the founder of Sexual Safety Australia, a workplace and school sexual-safety educator specialist. Her work includes early-intervention education in schools and whole-community prevention approaches. She is known for systems-based thinking, ethical clarity, and prevention-focused practice. With qualifications in teaching and human resources, she delivers training and consultation that support organisations to move beyond compliance toward meaningful prevention. Tracy is currently completing a Master of Counselling and training in Men's Behaviour Change Program facilitation. By the end of 2026, she will practise as a psychotherapist alongside her education and prevention work.

Born in Brisbane and based in Sydney, Tracy lives close to the ocean, drawing energy from nature and time with her family. She has a deep love of literature, a lifelong connection to animals, and a grounded lifestyle reflecting the same values she brings to her work: presence, care, and integrity.

LinkedIn: www.linkedin.com/in/tracy-sedman-sexual-safety-australia-50858613a

Website: www.tracysedman.com.au

Website: www.sexualsafetyaustralia.com.au